GUNMARKS

Books by David Byron

GUNMARKS
THE FIREARMS PRICE GUIDE

GUNMARKS
DAVID BYRON

A HERBERT MICHELMAN BOOK

Crown Publishers, Inc., New York

This book is dedicated to

Jeannie Ferrin

for the artwork in this book

and for her patience.

© 1979 by David Byron
All rights reserved. No part of this book may be reproduced or utilized in any form or by any means, electronic or mechanical, including photocopying, recording, or by any information storage and retrieval system, without permission in writing from the publisher.
Inquiries should be addressed to Crown Publishers, Inc., One Park Avenue, New York, N.Y. 10016.

Printed in the United States of America

Published simultaneously in Canada by
General Publishing Company Limited

Library of Congress Cataloging in Publication Data

Byron, David.
  Gunmarks.

  "A Herbert Michelman book."
  Includes index.
  1. Firearms—Collectors and collecting. 2. Firearms—Identification. 3. Firearms—Trade-marks. I. Title.
TS532.4.B96   1979   683'.4'0275   79-20339
ISBN 0-517-53848-2

CONTENTS

MARKS	1	Stars	61
Monograms in circles	1	Transportation and Buildings	63
Monograms in ovals	9	Various Inanimate Objects	64
Monograms in various borders	13	Geometric Designs	65
Monograms without borders	14	Birds	70
Letters in circles	17	Hearts	74
Numbers in circles	25	Lions	75
Letters in ovals	26	Dogs	78
Letters in diamonds	30	Horses	79
Letters in triangles	31	Bears	80
Letters in rectangles	32	Insects	80
Letters in various borders	34	Deer	81
Letters without borders	41	Buffalo	81
Numbers without borders	43	Various Animals	82
Anchors	44	Humans	83
Arrows	45	Plants	86
Bombs	47	Crests	88
Crosses	48		
Bullets and Guns	49	NAMES AND CODES	95
Crowns	51	INDEX	181

INTRODUCTION

Perhaps the fastest-growing field of collector interest in this country is firearms and for a good reason. Guns have a unique place in American history and folklore. For instance it's hard to think of Colt without remembering the Old West, or of Daniel Boone without his "Kentucky" rifle. This strong association with our heritage is spurring a growing interest even among people who don't consider themselves "gun nuts" but who do want a tangible link with their past.

This intense interest has made the well-known arms scarce and expensive, and has led the collectors and speculators to the relatively undefined group of cartridge arms from the smaller makers.

For years as a retail gun dealer and collector I spent hours trying to identify guns with strange names and marks, and while there were a few good reference books about flintlock and percussion arms, information concerning cartridge arms was scarce. Out of frustration I have compiled this book listing about three thousand names and codes from A.A. to Zonda, and one thousand trademarks and proofs found on guns made since 1870. This covers the myriad of guns made in the U.S. and abroad but like all works of this type cannot cover the entire spectrum. There are still scores of names and marks that haven't been ascribed to any particular marker, and for space economy I have left out these as well as descriptions of a few very well known firms. It is my hope that in time most of the unknowns can be defined.

This book is divided into two main sections, the first being devoted to marks and is subdivided by visual pattern. The second is an alpha-numeric listing of names and codes.

The information in this book has been gathered from reliable sources and is believed to be accurate. I especially want to thank Ken King and Bill Mrock of Orlando, Florida, Frank Moyer of Philadelphia, Pennsylvania, and Charles Meyer of Sanford, Florida, for their tremendous assistance with my research.

MARKS

Monograms in circles

 Armero Especialistas Reunidas of Eibar, Spain trademark on revolvers.

 Hopkins & Allen of Norwich, Conn. gripmark on revolvers.

 Jose Aldazabal of Eibar, Spain trademark on pistol.

Domingo Acha y Cia. gripmark on Looking Glass pistols.

 American Arms Co. of Boston, Mass. gripmark on revolvers.

 Retolaza Hermanos of Eibar, Spain gripmark.

 Andrew Fryberg & Co. of Hopkinton, Mass. gripmark on revolvers.

 S.A. Vincitor of Eibar, Spain gripmark.

 Alois Tomiska of Pilsen, Czechoslovakia gripmark on "Little Tom" pistol.

 Trocaola, Aranzabal y. Cia. of Eibar, Spain trademark on T.A.C. revolvers.

1

Monograms in circles

Isidro Gaztanaga of Eibar, Spain trademark on pistols.

J. Cesar Trade Mark on pistols made by Tomas de Urizar Eibar, Spain.

Hijos de C. Arrizabalaga of Eibar, Spain gripmark.

Garate, Anitua y Cia. of Eibar, Spain gripmark on "Express" pistols.

Fab. d'Armes F. Delu of Liege, Belgium gripmark on Delu pistols.

Bauer Firearms Co. of Fraser, Mich. trademark.

Domingo Acha y Cia of Ermua, Spain on Looking Glass pistol.

Crucelegui Hermanos of Eibar, Spain gripmark on pistols.

Etxezaraga Abitua y Cia. of Eibar, Spain gripmark on pistols.

Esperanza y Unceta, Guernica, Spain, gripmark on Victoria pistol.

Beistegui Hermanos of Eibar, Spain trademark on handguns.

Monograms in circles

 Fabbrica Nazionale d'Armi of Brescia, Italy trademark on rifles and shotguns.

 U. S. ordnance inspection mark of G. H. Stewart on M1911 pistols.

 Georg Grabner of Austria gripmark on 3mm Kolibri pistols.

 Orbea Hermanos of Eibar, Spain trademark on handguns.

 J. Jacquemart of Herstal, Belgium gripmark on pistols.

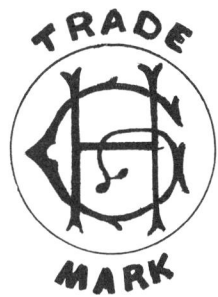 Guisasola Hermanos of Eibar, Spain.

 Mre. d'Armes des Pyrenees Francaises of Hendaye, France trademark.

 Firearms Import & Export of Miami, Fla. gripmark on pistols.

 Gabilondo y Cia of Elgoibar, Spain trademark.

 Hijos de Calixto Arrizabalaga of Eibar, Spain on "Sharp Shooter" pistol. (Note spelling.)

Monograms in circles

 Maltby-Henley Co. of New York trademark.

 Iver Johnson of Fitchburg, Mass. gripmark on revolvers.

 Hy Hunter of Hollywood, Cal. gripmark.

 Fab. d'Armes Jannsen et Fills of Liege, Belgium, trademark.

 Gregorio Bolumburo of Eibar, Spain gripmark on Gloria pistols.

 Theodor Kommer, Suhl, Germany gripmark on Model II pistol.

 Gevelot et Gaupillat of Paris, France trademark.

 Dutch Colonial Forces mark on Luger pistols.

Monograms in circles

 Fab. d'Armes de Grande Precision gripmark on Minerve pistols.

 Maltby-Curtis Co. of New York City gripmark on revolvers.

 U. S. ordnance inspection mark of J. M. Gilbert on M1911 pistols.

 Meriden Firearms Co. of Meriden, Conn. trademark.

 August Menz of Suhl, Germany trademark on pistols.

 U. S. ordnance inspection mark of W. H. Gorton on M1911 pistols.

 Meriden Firearms Co. of Meriden, Conn. trademark on revolvers.

 Fernando Ormachea of Ermua, Spain gripmark.

 J. Bertrand of Liege, Belgium trademark.

 Mre. Francaise d'Armes et Cycles of St. Etienne, France trademark.

5

Monograms in circles

 Ojanguren y Marcaide of Eibar, Spain used on revolvers.

 Sears, Roebuck & Co. gripmark on revolvers.

 Heinrich Ortgies & Co. of Erfurt, Germany, gripmark on pistols.

 Retolaza Hermanos of Eibar, Spain gripmark on pistols.

 Friederich Pickert of Zella-Mehlis, Germany trademark.

 Smith & Wesson of Springfield, Mass. trademark.

 Spanish Government Acceptance Mark.

 Suinaga y Aramperri of Eibar, Spain trademark on revolvers.

 Amadeo Rossi & Co. of Sao Leopoldo, Brazil.

 J. P. Sauer u. Sohn trademark as found on Model H-38 pistols, ca. 1940.

Monograms in circles

 J. P. Sauer u. Sohn of West Germany trademark.

 Trocaola, Aranabal y Cia of Eibar, Spain gripmark on revolver.

 Thompson/Center Arms Co. of Rochester, N. H. trademark.

 Russian quality control mark.

 Tokyo Gas & Electric of Japan trademark on pistols.

 Metallurgica Bresciana of Brescia, Italy trademark on revolvers.

 Ojanguren y Vidosa of Eibar, Spain trademark.

 Russian quality control mark.

 U. S. ordnance inspection mark of W. G. Penfield on M1911 pistols.

Monograms in circles

 Carl Walther Waffenfabrik of Zella-Mehlis, Germany gripmark.

 Ceska Zbrojovka of Strakonice, Czechoslovakia gripmark.

 Davis-Warner Arms Corp. of Assonet, Mass. gripmark on infallible pistol.

 Ceska Zbrojovka of Strakonice, Czechoslovakia gripmark.

 Weiner Waffenfabrik, Vienna, Austria gripmark on "Little Tom" pistols.

 Zaragoza gripmark on Corla pistol.

Monograms in ovals

 Acha Hermanos of Ermua, Spain gripmark.

 Frommer of Budapest, Hungary gripmark on "Baby" pistol.

 August Menz of Suhl, Germany gripmark.

 Frommer of Budapest, Hungary gripmark on "Liliput" pistol.

 Berastain y Cia. of Eibar, Spain gripmark on Bufalo pistol.

 Frommer of Budapest, Hungary gripmark on "Stop" pistol.

 Becker & Hollander of Suhl, Germany trademark on pistols.

 Firma Pfannl of Krems/Donau, Austria gripmark on Erika pistol.

 Henrion et Dassy of Liege, Belgium trademark on pistols.

 Fab. National d'Armes de Guerre of Herstal, Belgium trademark.

Monograms in ovals

 Fabrique Nationale d'Armes de Guerre of Herstal, Belgium gripmark on pistols.

 Hourat et Vie, Pau, France gripmark on pistols.

DANTON

 Gabilondo y Cia of Elgoibar, Spain trademark.

 Hopkins & Allen trademark on buttplates.

 Guisasola Hermanos of Eibar, Spain gripmark on pistols.

 Isidro Gaztanaga of Eibar, Spain trademark.

 E. Zehner of Suhl, Germany trademark.

 Gabilondo y Cia of Elgoibar, Spain trademark on pistols.

 French blackpowder ordinary proof (Paris).

 Armand Gauage of Liege, Belgium trademark.

 French blackpowder double proof mark (Paris).

10

Monograms in ovals

Echave y Arizmendi of Eibar, Spain gripmark on Bronco pistols.

Nicolas Pieper of Herstal, Belgium gripmark on pistols.

Bernardon-Martin of St. Etienne, France gripmark on Hermetic pistols.

Robar et Dekerkhove of Liege, Belgium trademark.

Erquiaga, Muguruza y Cia. of Eibar Spain gripmark on Fiel #1 pistol.

Rheinische Metallwaren u. Maschinenfabrik of Sommerda, Germany (Rheinmetall) gripmark on Dreyse pistols.

Societe Francaise d'Armes de St. Etienne, of France trademark on pistol.

Societe d'Armes of Paris, France gripmark on pistol.

Oesterreichische Waffenfabrik Ges. of Steyr, Austria trademark on pistol.

Modesto Santos of Eibar, Spain gripmark on Action pistols.

Monograms in ovals

 Iraola, Salaverria of Eibar, Spain gripmark on pistols.

 Russian quality control mark.

 J. Bertrand of Liege, Belgium gripmark.

 Carl Waltehr of Zella-St. Blasit, Germany trademark.

 Fab. d'Armes de Grande Precision of Spain gripmark on Minerve pistol.

 C.G. Haenel, Suhl, Germany, gripmark on First Model Schmeisser pistol.

 Winchester Repeating Arms Co. monogram on lever-action shotguns.

Monograms in various borders

 Lothar Walther of Konigsbronn, W. Germany.

 Azanza y Arrizabalaga of Eibar, Spain trademark on pistols.

 Auguste Francotte of Liege, Belgium gripmark on pistols.

 Remington Arms Co. of Ilion, N. Y. gripmark on revolvers.

 Larranga y Elartza of Eibar, Spain trademark on pistol.

 Hispano Argentina Fab. de Automoviles of Buenos Aires trademark on HAFDASA pistols.

 Waffenfabrik Mauser of Oberndorf, Germany trademark on pistols.

 Charles Ph. Clement of Liege, Belgium trademark.

 Mauser Werke of Oberndorf, Germany trademark.

 Antonio Errasti of Eibar, Spain trademark on pistols.

Monograms without borders

 Sweden proof firing mark.

 Austro-Hungarian and Czechoslovakian black-powder proof for Prague 1891-1931.

 Sweden final inspection mark since 1962.

 Austro-Hungarian and Austrian 1st proof for Ferlach since 1891.

 English R.S.A.F. Enfield mark on Bren guns.

 Austro-Hungarian and Austrian 1st proof for Vienna since 1891.

 G. C. Dornheim of Suhl, Germany trademark.

 Austro-Hungarian and Czechoslovakian smokeless powder proof for Weipert 1891-1931.

 Deutsche Waffen u. Munitionsfabriken of Berlin, Germany, trademark.

 Belgian provisional black-powder proof since 1852.

 Erma Werke Munchen of Dachau, W. Germany trademark on pistols.

Monograms without borders

 Gustav Genschow & Co. of Berlin, Germany trademark.

 Austro-Hungarian and Austrian smokeless powder proof since 1891 for Vienna.

 Austro-Hungarian and Czechoslovakian smokeless powder proof for Weipert 1891-1931.

 Hecker & Koch of Oberndorf/Neckar, West Germany.

 Swiss military proof.

 A. Krauser Waffenfabrik of Zella-Mehlis, Germany gripmark on Helfricht Model 3 pistols.

 Parker-Hale Ltd. of Birmingham, England trademark.

 Austro-Hungarian and Hungarian smokeless powder proof for Budapest 1891-1928.

 Relay Products (Pty.) Ltd. of Johannesburg, South Africa makers of Mamba pistols.

 Austro-Hungarian and Austrian smokeless powder proof 1891 to date for Ferlach.

 Austro-Hungarian and Czechoslovakian smokeless powder proof for Prague 1891-1931.

 Romerwerk of Suhl, Germany gripmark on pistol.

Monograms without borders

 Security Industries of America of Little Ferry, N.J. trademark on revolvers.

 Warner Arms Corp. of Norwich, Conn. trademark on infallible pistol.

 Sterling Arms Corp. of Lockport, N.Y. trademark on pistols.

 Winchester Repeating Arms trademark.

 Union Switch & Signal of Swissvale, Pa. trademark on M1911A1 pistols.

 French mark on Mauser HSC's made in France.

 East German "first quality" mark.

Letters in circles

 S. A. Alkartasua of Guernica, Spain trademark on pistols.

 K. Burgsmuller Sen. of Kreiensen, West Germany trademark on revolvers.

 Armi Galesi of Brescia, Italy trademark.

 Pietro Beretta of Brescia, Italy trademark.

 American Arms Co. of Boston, Mass. gripmark.

 Portuguese mark on Guedes rifles.

 Theodor Bergmann of Gaggenau, Germany gripmark on Model 3 pistol.

 Deutsche Werke of Erfurt, Germany trademark.

 Rohm Gesellschaft of Sontheim/Brenz, West Germany revolver gripmark.

 Herman Weihrauch Sportwaffenfabrik gripmark on revolvers.

 Bernedo y Cia. of Eibar, Spain gripmark on pistols.

 F. Dusek of Opocno, Czechoslovakia gripmark on .25 pistols.

Letters in circles

 Echave, Arizmendi y Cia of Eibar, Spain trademark.

 Erma Waffenfabrik trademark.

 EIG Corp. trademark on revolvers made in Italy.

 Austrian definitive proof on arms of foreign make 1929-40.

 EIG trademark on Rohm revolvers.

 Rohm Gesellschaft of Sontheim/Brenz, West Germany gripmark on revolvers.

 EIG of Miami, Florida trademark on imported guns.

 Firearms International of Washington, D. C. trademark.

 EIG of Miami, Florida trademark on imported guns.

 Gertenberger & Eberwein of Gussenstadt, Germany.

 Spesco of Atlanta, Ga. gripmark on pistols.

 Schmidt & Haberman of Suhl, Germany trademark on sporting arms.

 Firearms Import & Export of Miami, Fla. trademark.

Letters in circles

 Fab. Material de Guerre del Ejercito of Santiago, Chile.

 Harrington & Richardson gripmark on revolvers.

 Gustloff Werke of Suhl, Germany gripmark on pistols.

 Harrington & Richardson of Gardner, Mass. gripmark on handguns.

 G.C. Dornheim of Suhl, Germany trademark.

 Herbert Schmidt of Ostheim, West Germany gripmark on revolvers.

 Rohm Gesellschaft of Sontheim/Brenz, West Germany revolver trademark on "Thalco's."

 High Standard Mfg. Co. of Hamden, Conn. gripmark on pistols.

 Hawes Firearms Co. of Van Nuys, Calif. gripmark.

 Hy Score Arms Co. of Brooklyn, N.Y. gripmark on Rohm revolvers.

 Russian final smokeless proof.

 Industria Armi Galesi of Brescia, Italy gripmark on Model 9 pistol.

 Hopkins & Allen of Norwich, Conn. trademark.

 H. Krieghoff of Ulm, West Germany trademark on shotguns.

19

Letters in circles

 J. G. Anschutz of Zella-Mehlis, Germany trademark.

 Nicolas Pieper gripmark on Legia pistol.

 J. M. Marlin of New Haven, Conn. trademark.

 Rohm Gesellschaft of Sontheim/Brenz, West Germany revolver gripmark.

 Henry M. Kolb of Philadelphia, Pa. gripmark on Baby Hammerless revolvers.

 Gabilondo y Cia. of Elgoibar, Spain gripmark on pistols.

 Russian shotgun patterning check mark.

 Francisco Arizmendi of Eibar, Spain gripmark on pistols.

 Gabilondo y Cia of Elgoibar, Spain trademark.

 Kriegskorte & Co. of Stuttgart, West Germany trademark on rifles.

 Gabilondo y Cia. of Elgoibar, Spain gripmark on pistols.

 Kriegeskorte & Co. of Stuttgart, West Germany trademark on rifles.

 Israeli definitive proof.

Letters in circles

 Tradewinds, Inc. of Tacoma, Wash. gripmark on Mercury pistols.

 Kirikkale Tufek Fb. of Kirikkale, Turkey trademark.

 Miroku trademark on buttplates.

 Mre. Stephanoise d'Armes St. Etienne, France trademark on shotguns and rifles.

 Martin A. Bascaran of Eibar, Spain gripmark on Martian pistols.

 Gerstenberger u. Eberwein of Gussenstadt, West Germany gripmark on revolvers.

 Precise Imports Corp. gripmark on imported pistols.

 Robar et Cie. of Liege, Belgium gripmark on Melior 1920 New Model.

 Precise Imports Corp. trademark on pistol grips.

 Robar et Cie. of Liege, Belgium on Melior 1920 (no safety).

 Precise Imports Corp. trademark on Rohm revolvers.

Letters in circles

 Rohm Gesellschaft of Sontheim/Brenz, West Germany on revolvers marked "Thalco Plinker."

 Rohm Gesellschaft of Sontheim/Brenz, West Germany revolver trademark.

 West Germany admission to proof of blank firing guns.

 Rohm Gesellschaft of Sontheim/Brenz, West Germany.

 E. Remington & Sons of Ilion, N.Y. gripmark on revolvers.

 Rigarmi of Brescia, Italy gripmark on pistols.

 Mre. d'Armes Automatiques Bayonne of Bayonne, France.

 Rohm Gesellschaft of Sontheim/Brenz, West Germany trademark on revolvers imported by Rosco Arms Co.

 Reck Sportwaffenfabrik of Nurnberg, Germany.

 Rohm Gesellschaft of Sontheim/Brenz, West Germany revolver gripmark.

 Remington Arms Co. of Ilion, N.Y. trademark.

 Rohm Gesellschaft of Sontheim/Brenz West Germany trademark on revolver.

Letters in circles

 Amadeo Rossi of S. Leopoldo, Brazil.

 Fred Bifflar & Co. of Chicago, Ill. gripmark on Secret Service Special revolvers.

 German Nazi party mark on Walther pistols (RZM).

 Rohm Gesellschaft of Sontheim/Brenz, West Germany gripmark on revolvers.

 Etablecimientos Venturini A.A.I.C.Y.F. of South America trademark.

 Smith & Wesson of Springfield, Mass. gripmark on revolvers.

 Gabilondo y Cia of Elgoibar, Spain trademark on revolver.

 Orueta Hermanos of Eibar, Spain trademark on revolvers.

 Gabilondo y Cia of Elgoibar Spain trademark on revolver.

 Taurus gripmark on revolvers made in Brazil.

 R. F. Sedgley of Philadelphia, Pa. gripmark on Baby Hammerless revolvers.

 T. E. Ryan of Norwich, Conn. gripmark on revolvers.

23

Letters in circles

 Mre. d'Armes des Pyrenees of Hendaye, France.

 Rohm Gesellschaft of Sontheim/Brenz, West Germany trademark on revolvers.

 Iver Johnson of Fitchburg, Mass. gripmark on U. S. Revolver Co. guns.

 Russian final black-powder proof (Tula).

 Gerstenberger u. Eberwein of Gussenstadt, West Germany gripmark on revolvers imported by Valor.

 Ceska Zbrojovka of Strakonice, Czechoslovakia gripmark on "Z" pistol.

 Rohm Gesellschaft of Sontheim/Brenz, West Germany gripmark on revolvers imported by Valor of Miami.

 Rohm Gesellschaft gripmark on revolvers imported by Rosco Arms Co.

 Rohm Gesellschaft trademark on revolvers imported by Stoeger Arms Corp.

 Herman Weirauch Sportwaffenfabrik, Zella-Mehlis, Germany trademark.

 Israeli definitive proof.

Numbers in circles

 Gerstenberger u. Eberwein of Gussenstadt, West Germany gripmark.

 Carl Walther of Zella-Mehlis, Germany gripmark on Mod. 8 pistol.

 Esprin Hermanos of Eibar, Spain gripmark on revolvers.

 August Menz of Suhl, Germany, gripmark on Model II pistol.

 August Menz, Suhl, Germany gripmark on Liliput pistol.

 Mre. d'Armes des Pyrenees gripmark on Nazi-issue Unique pistols.

 August Menz of Suhl, Germany gripmark.

 Echave y Arizmendi of Eibar, Spain gripmark.

 Russian provisional black-powder proof (Tula).

Letters in ovals

 Auguste Francotte of Liege, Belgium trademark.

 Colt Firearms trademark on revolvers, ca. 1920.

 Arizmendi y Zulaica of Eibar, Spain.

 Trocaola y Aranzabal of Eibar, Spain gripmark on revolver.

 Theodor Bergman of Suhl, Germany gripmark on pistols.

 East German Suhl proof House.

 Berlin-Suhler Waffen trademark on sporting arms.

 Echave, Arizmendi y Cia of Eibar, Spain trademark.

 Belgian pressure barrel proof mark.

 Emil Eckoldt of Suhl, Germany trademark on rifles.

 Charles Ph. Clement, Liege, Belgium Gripmark on pistols.

 Echave, Arizmendi y Cia. of Eibar, Spain gripmark.

Letters in ovals

 Belgian black-powder proof since 1810.

 Marlin Firearm Co. of New Haven, Conn. trademark and proof.

 Esperanza y Unceta of Guernica, Spain (Astra) trademark on early pistols.

 Theodor Kommer of Zella-Mehlis, Germany gripmark on Model III pistol.

 Spanish Mod. 1921 Pistol Same as Astra 400.

 Fritz Mann of Suhl, Germany trademark on pistol.

 Gabilondo y Cia. of Elgoibar, Spain trademark.

 Productos Mendoza of Mexico City, Mexico.

 Gotthilf von Nordheim of Mehlis, Germany trademark.

 Fabbrica E. Woerther of Buenos Aires, Argentina gripmark.

 Jager & Co. of Suhl, Germany trademark on pistols.

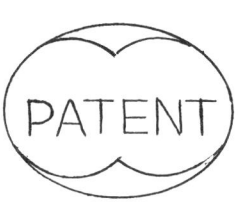 Fab. d'Armes de Guerre of Eibar, Spain trademark.

Letters in ovals

 Pietro Beretta of Brescia, Italy trademark.

 Ruby Arms Co. of Elgoibar, Spain gripmark on pistols.

 J.P. Sauer & Sohn of Suhl, Germany gripmark on pistols.

 Zbrojovka Praga of Prague, Czechoslovakia trademark on pistols.

 Sauer & Sohn, V.C. Schilling, and C.G. Haenel of Suhl, Germany trademark on ordnance revolvers.

 Posumavska Zbrojovka Kdyne of Czechoslovakia.

 Soc. Espanola de Armas y Municiones, Eibar, Spain gripmark.

 Gabilondo y Cia. of Elgoibar, Spain gripmark on Ruby Arms Co. pistols.

 Schweitzer Industrie Gesellschaft of Switzerland trademark.

 Gabilondo y Cia of Elgoibar, Spain trademark on revolver.

 Stenda Werke Waffenfabrik of Suhl, Germany trademark on pistols.

 Gabilondo y Urresti of Eibar, Spain trademark on pistol.

 South African proof mark.

Letters in ovals

 Esperanza y Unceta of Guernica, Spain trademark on Union pistol.

 Verney-Carron of St. Etienne, France gripmark on pistols made for them by M. Seytres.

 Vincenzo Bernardelli of Brescia, Italy trademark.

 Hijos de A. Echeverria of Eibar, Spain gripmark on pistols.

 V. Bernardelli of Brescia, Italy trademark.

 V. Charles Schilling & C.G. Haenel of Suhl, Germany trademark on ordnance revolvers.

 Webley and Scott, Ltd. of Birmingham, England gripmark.

29

Letters in diamonds

 Mre. d'Armes des Pyrenees of Hendaye, France gripmark on pistols.

 Fritz Langenhan of Zella-Mehlis, Germany gripmark on Model III pistol.

 Russian provisional black-powder proof (Izhevsk).

 Fritz Langenhan of Zella-Mehlis, Germany gripmark on Model II pistol.

 Howa Machinery, Ltd. of Tokyo, Japan trademark.

 F. Dusek of Opocno, Czechoslovakia trademark.

 Russian quality control mark.

 Darlick Corporation of Hamden, Conn. trademark.

 American Import Co. of San Francisco, Calif. trademark.

 Austro-Hungarian and Hungarian 2nd proof for Budapest 1891-1928.

Letters in triangles

 Christopher Funk of Suhl, Germany trademark.

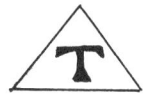 Russian Tula proof mark.

 Fabryka Bronn Radom. of Radom, Poland gripmark on "Radom" pistol.

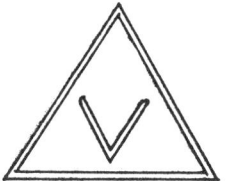 Sweden — cold-bored steel barrel mark.

 L. Ancion-Marx of Liege, Belgium trademark on revolvers.

 Fabryka Bronn Radom of Radom, Poland gripmark on "Radom" pistol.

 Russian Tula proof mark.

 East German "good quality" mark.

 East German "special quality" mark.

 Hungarian second proof for unfinished barrels 1929-71.

 Sharps Arms Co. of Salt Lake City, Utah trademark.

 East German "utility quality" mark.

Letters in rectangles

 French proof on foreign made arms (Paris).

 Czechoslovakian proof mark on gas guns from 1962.

 French proof on foreign made arms (St. Etienne).

 Etablissments Darne of St. Etienne, France trademark on shotguns.

 Deutsche Waffen u. Munitions fabriken of Berlin, Germany trademark.

 Mre. d'Armes des Pyrenees of Hendaye, France gripmark.

 Fabrica de Material de Guerre of Santiago, Chile gripmark on pistols.

 Anciens Etablissments Pieper of Herstal, Belgium, gripmark on pistols.

 Henrion, Dassy & Heuschen of Liege, Belgium.

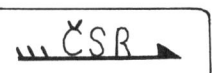 Theodor Bergmann of Gaggenau, Germany trademark.

 Theodor Kommer, Zella-Mehlis, Germany gripmark on Model II pistol.

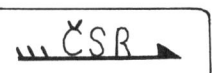 Czechoslovakian proof mark on gas guns 1955-62.

 Puccinelli Company of San Anselmo, Calif. trademark on shotguns.

Letters in rectangles

Retolaza Hermanos of Eibar, Spain gripmark on pistols.

Reck Sportwaffenfabrik of West Germany, trademark.

Mre. d'Armes LePage of Liege, Belgium gripmark.

Azanza y Arrizabalaga of Eibar, Spain gripmark.

Akt. Gesellschaft Lignose of Berlin, Germany trademark on pistol.

Sheridan Products, Inc. of Racine, Wisc. gripmark.

French mark indicating standard dimensions (St. Etienne).

Sabatti & Tanfoglid of Brescia, Italy trademark.

Perla gripmark on pistols made in Czechoslovakia.

Waffenfabriken Simson & Co. of Suhl, Germany gripmark on pistol.

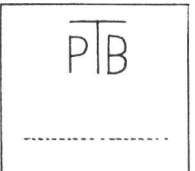
West German admission to proof for long guns and barrel inserts.

Stenda Werke Waffenfabrik of Suhl, Germany trademark.

Letters in various borders

 Oesterreichische Waffenfabriks Ges of Steyr, Austria gripmark.

 Oesterreichische Werke Anstalt of Vienna, Austria gripmark.

 Franz Stock of Berlin, Germany gripmark on pistols.

 Mre. d'Armes des Pyrenees of Hendaye, France trademark on pistols.

 Mre. d'Armes des Pyrenees of Hendaye, France trademark.

 Waffenfabrik Mauser of Oberndorf, Germany trademark.

 A. Zoli of Brescia, Italy trademark.

 Deutsche Waffen u. Munitionsfabriken trademark.

 Triple-S Development Co., Inc. of Wickliffe, Ohio trademark on rifles.

 Oesterreichische Werke Anstalt of Vienna, Austria trademark.

 Ernesto Breda of Milan, Italy trademark.

Letters in various borders

 Fab. Nationale d'Armes de Guerre of Herstal, Belgium gripmark on Baby Browning pistol.

 Israeli mark on arms for export.

 Astra-Unceta y Cia. of Guernica, Spain gripmark.

 Orbea Hermanos of Eibar, Spain gripmark on Orbea .25 pistol.

 C. G. Haenel of Suhl, Germany trademark.

 Astra-Unceta y Cia of Guernica, Spain gripmark.

 A. Vilimec of Kdyne, Czechoslovakia gripmark.

 Kirikale Tufek Fb. of Kirikale, Turkey gripmark.

 Albin Wahl, Zella-Mehlis, Germany, gripmark on Stern pistol.

 Israeli mark on arms for export.

 Western Arms Corporation of Los Angeles, Calif. gripmark (later Winfield Arms Corp.).

 Pietro Beretta of Brescia, Italy.

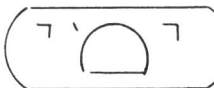 Israeli proof on small arms.

 Mre. d'Armes Automatiques Bayone, France gripmark on pistols.

 Israeli current proof mark.

Letters in various borders

 Tomas de Urizar y Cia of Eibar, Spain trademark.

 Garate, Anitua y Cia. of Eibar, Spain gripmark on pistols.

 J. Bertrand of Liege, Belgium trademark.

 Hijos de Calixto Arrizabalaga of Eibar, Spain trademark on pistol.

 Mre. d'Armes des Pyrenees of Hendaye, France trademark.

 R. S. Industria Obrera Armera of Eibar, Spain trademark on pistol.

 Gaztenaga, Trocaola y Ibarzabal of Eibar, Spain trademark.

 Robar et Cie of Liege, Belgium gripmark on Melior M1920.

 Echave y Arizmendi of Eibar, Spain gripmark on Vite Model 1913.

 Martin A. Bascaran, Eibar, Spain gripmark on pistol.

 Carl Walther of Ulm/Donau, West Germany trademark.

 Tomas de Urizar y Cia of Eibar, Spain gripmark.

Letters in various borders

 Tomas de Urizar y Cia of Eibar, Spain gripmark.

 Arizmendi y Goenaga of Eibar, Spain gripmark on pistols.

 Arizmendi y Goenaga, Eibar, Spain gripmark on pistols.

 Francisco Arizmendi of Eibar, Spain trademark on pistols.

 Bestegui Hermanos trademark on .32 pistols made for Fab. d'Armes de Grande Precision of Eibar, Spain, ca. 1920.

 Forehand & Wadsworth of Worcester, Mass. gripmark on revolvers.

 Martin A. Bascaran of Eibar, Spain gripmark on pistols.

 Otis A. Smith of Rock Falls, Conn. gripmark on revolvers.

 Francisco Arizmendi of Eibar, Spain gripmark.

 Bonifacio Echeverria of Eibar, Spain trademark.

 Turner & Ross of Boston, Mass. gripmark on revolvers.

Letters in various borders

 J. G. Anschutz of Ulm, West Germany trademark.

 West German mark on guns that fire ammunition that develop less than 5.5 ft. lb. of energy.

 Spanish voluntary smokeless shotgun proof 1929-31.

 G. C. Dornheim of Suhl, Germany trademark.

 Bernhard Paatz of Zella-Mehlis, Germany trademark on rifles.

 Gevelot S. A. of Paris, France trademark on rifles.

 Charles Ph. Clement of Liege, Belgium on M1903 pistol.

 Russian final smokeless proof.

 Apaolozo Hermanos of Zumorraga, Spain gripmark.

 Spanish re-enforced smokeless shotgun proof 1929-31.

C. G. Haenel
Suhl

C. G. Haenel Waffenfabrik of Suhl, Germany trademark on pistols.

Letters in various borders

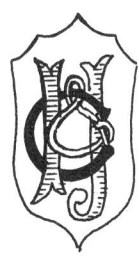 Iver Johnson of Fitchburg, Mass. trademark on shotguns.

 Mikroku Firearms Mfg. Co. Ltd. of Kochi, Japan Trademark on shotguns.

 Russian quality control mark.

 Marlin Arms Co. trademark on buttplates, ca. 1900.

 Weiner Waffenfabrik, Vienna, Austria gripmark on "Little Tom" pistols.

 Rivolier Pere et Fils of St. Etienne, France trademark.

 Lasagabaster Hermanos of Eibar, Spain gripmark on Douglas pistol.

 Marlin Firearms Co. of New Haven, Conn. gripmark on revolvers.

 J. Stevens Arms & Tool Co. trademark on buttplates.

Letters in various borders

 Tula Weapons Factory, Tula, Russia gripmark on "Toz" pistol.

 Russian final black-powder proof (Izhevsk).

 Valtion Kivaari Tehdas of Tourola-Jyvaskyla, Finland gripmark on Lahti pistols.

Letters without borders

 S. A. Alkartasuna of Guernica, Spain trademark on pistols.

 Ithaca Gun Co. of Ithaca, N.Y. trademark on buttplates.

 B.R.F. trademark on .25 cal. South African pistols.

 LA Distributors of New York City trademark.

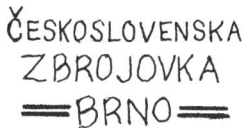 Zbrojovka Brno of Brno, Czechoslovakia on Mauser rifle.

 Fritz Mann of Suhl, Germany trademark on pistols.

 Spanish voluntary proof for shotguns 1923-25.

 Konout & Spol. of Kdyne, Czechoslovakia gripmark on Mars .25 pistol.

 Firearms Import & Export of Miami, Fla. gripmark on pistols.

 Robar et DeKerkhove of Liege, Belgium gripmark on Melior Old Model.

 Iver Johnson of Fitchburg, Mass. gripmark on revolvers.

 O. F. Mossberg & Sons, Inc. of New Haven, Conn. trademark on rifles and shotguns.

Letters without borders

 Soc. Francaise de Metallurgie et de Mecanique of Paris, France trademark on shotguns.

 Rohm Gesellschaft of Sontheim/Brenz, West Germany gripmark on handguns.

 Noble Mfg. Co. of Haydenville, Mass. trademark.

 Theodor Bergmann of Gaggenau, Germany trademark on pistols.

 Phoenix Arms Co. of Lowell, Mass. trademark on pistols.

 Franz Stock trademark on .32 pistols.

 Zbrojovka Praga, Prague, Czechoslovakia, gripmark on pistol.

УИA Russian choke indication - cylinder.

 Austrian superior smokeless proof 1929-40.

 Venus Waffenwerk, Zella-Mehlis, Germany, trademark on pistols.

 RG Industries of Miami, Fla. trademark.

ЧОК Russian choke indication - full.

Numbers without borders

Я   Swiss rejection mark.

   Israeli definitive proof.

БУМ   Russian mark on shotguns meaning "paper shotshells only."

   German gripmark signifying pistols chambered for 9mm Parabellum.

π- 40K   Russian choke indication - modified.

   Swiss rejection mark.

Anchors

 French Naval Acceptance Mark.

 Gregorio Bolumburu of Eibar, Spain gripmark on Marina pistol.

 Hood Firearms Co. of Norwich, Conn. trademark on Victoria revolvers.

 Maisuru Arsenal, Japan mark on handguns.

 French Naval Acceptance Mark.

 German Weimar naval acceptance mark.

 Kure Arsenal, Japan marking on handguns.

 Portuguese Naval Acceptance Mark.

 Navy Arms trademark.

 Auguste Francotte of Liege, Belgium trademark.

 Regia Marina — Italian navy acceptance mark.

 Portuguese naval acceptance mark.

 H. Krieghoff of Suhl, Germany trademark on Luger pistols.

 Portuguese naval crest.

 Toyokawa Arsenal, Japan mark on handguns.

 Sasebo Arsenal, Japan mark on handguns.

 Yokosuka Arsenal, Japan mark on handguns.

Arrows

 English military acceptance mark.

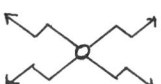 French special mark for arms ready for delivery when proofed (St. Etienne).

 West German proof, Kiel.

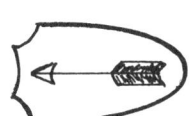 Russian Izhevsk proof mark.

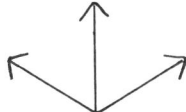 French special mark for arms ready for delivery when proofed (Paris).

 Russian Izhevsk proof mark.

Arrows

 P. Beretta of Brescia, Italy gripmark on pistols.

 English military mark meaning equipment is obsolete.

 Pietro Beretta of Brescia, Italy trademark.

 Czechoslovakian mark on foreign made firearms.

 Pietro Beretta of Brescia, Italy.

 Czechoslovakian mark on stud drivers.

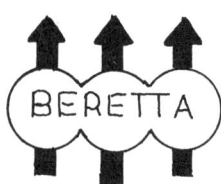 P. Beretta of Brescia, Italy trademark.

 Czechoslovakian mark on foreign made firearms.

 Czechoslovakian mark.

 Fab d'Armes Jannsen et Fils of Liege, Belgium trademark.

 Antonio Zoli trademark on buttplates.

Bombs

 Spanish definitive proof on rifles 1929-31.

 Spanish final revolver proof.

 U. S. military acceptance mark.

 Belgian proof mark on guns of foreign make since 1924.

 Soc. Espanola de Armas y Municiones of Eibar, Spain, trademark on pistols.

 Spanish definitive proof on foreign arms.

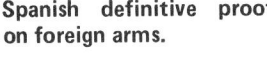

 Spanish definitive black-powder proof for breech-loading rifled arms 1923-25.

 Spanish final pistol proof mark.

 Spanish definitive black-powder proof for double barreled rifled breech-loaders 1923-25.

Crosses

 Swiss military acceptance mark.

 Swiss government ordnance acceptance mark.

 Swiss Government Acceptance Mark.

 Swiss military acceptance mark.

 Hämmerli of Lenzburg, Switzerland trademark.

 Swiss military acceptance mark.

Bullets and Guns

 Arizmendi y Goenaga of Spain gripmark on Teuf-Teuf pistols.

 Russian military acceptance mark.

 Mre. d'Armes Le Page of Liege, Belgium trademark.

 Albrecht Kind of Berlin-Nurnberg, Germany trademark.

 H. Krieghoff of Ulm, West Germany trademark.

 Connecticut Valley Arms, Inc. of Haddam, Conn. trademark.

 High Standard Sporting Firearms of Hamden, Conn. Trademark.

 Dakin Gun Co. trademark.

 Webley & Scott of Birmingham, England trademark.

 Fabrique Nationale of Herstal, Belgium gripmark on M1900 pistol.

 Greifelt & Co. of Suhl, Germany trademark on sporting arms.

 Theodor Bergmann of Suhl, Germany trademark on pistols.

 Jose Cruz Mugica of Eibar, Spain trademark.

 Webley & Scott of Birmingham, England trademark.

 Pretoria Arms Factory of South Africa.

 Webley & Scott of Birmingham, England trademark.

 A. W. Schwarzlose of Berlin, Germany trademark.

 Spanish definitive proof on single barrel black-powder shotguns 1923-25.

 S-M Corp. of Alexandria, Va. trademark on pistol.

 Spanish definitive black-powder proof on shotguns 1929-31.

Crowns

 Danish barrel proof after 1933.

 Auguste Francotte of Liege, Belgium trademark.

 Sweden Husqvarna barrel-mark.

 Auguste Francotte of Liege, Belgium trademark.

 Spanish definitive proof for blackpowder breech-loading shotguns since 1910.

 Auguste Francotte of Liege, Belgium trademark.

 German pistol and revolver proof, ca. 1891.

 Auguste Francotte of Liege, Belgium trademark.

  Italian provisional proof for unfinished arms 1930-51.

 Auguste Francotte of Liege, Belgium trademark.

 Azanza y Arrizabalaga of Eibar, Spain trademark on pistols.

 Arizmendi y Goenaga of Eibar, Spain trademark on pistols.

Crowns

	French smokeless proof on center-fire rifles (Paris).		English definitive black-powder proof (Birmingham).
	French smokeless proof on rifles (St. Etienne).		English smokeless proof (Birmingham) on rifles of foreign make since 1925.
	Berasaluze Areitio Aurtena y Cia. of Eibar, Spain gripmark on Allies pistol.		English definitive black-powder proof (Birmingham) on foreign arms since 1925.
	German proof using Mauser M-71 powder, ca. 1891.		English definitive black-powder proof (Birmingham).
	Belgian army ownership mark.		English blackpowder inspection mark (Birmingham) on foreign arms since 1925.
	English definitive proof (London) since 1925.		English inspection mark (Birmingham).

Crowns

 Spanish final smokeless proof mark on shotguns.

 Carl Gustaf trademark and proof on rifles.

 Danish barrel proof after 1933.

 Esperanza y Unceta, Guernica, Spain gripmark on Campo Giro pistols.

 German Danzig Arsenal Mark.

 Auguste Lebeau-Courally of Liege, Belgium trademark.

 German express rifle proof 1891-1939.

 Portuguese military mark on Mauser-Vergueiro rifles.

 Beistegui Hermanos of Eibar, Spain trademark on Libia pistols.

 Crown City Arms of Cortland, N.Y. trademark.

 English definitive black-powder proof (Birmingham) from 1813 to 1904.

 Egyptian Coat of Arms.

Crowns

 English definitive proof (London) since 1925.

 Husqvarna of Sweden trademark.

 English definitive black-powder proof (London) since 1637.

 Danish armory mark of Haerens Vaabenarsenalet.

 India proof mark 1907-50.

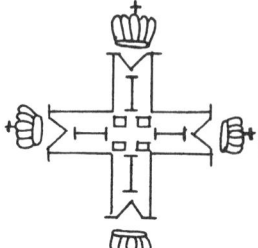 Roumanian mark of King Michael I on military arms.

 Husqvarna factory mark on rifles.

 Dutch government ownership mark.

 Sweden nitro proof.

 Husqvarna Vapenfabriks Aktiebolag of Husqvarna, Sweden gripmark on "Lahti" pistol.

 Austro-Hungarian and Hungarian proof mark 1891-1928.

Crowns

 Belgian double provisional proof.

 Spanish blackpowder proof on shotguns, final for muzzle-loaders, and second for breechloaders.

 Belgian triple provisional proof.

 French blackpowder definitive proof (St. Etienne).

 Belgian proof mark for definitive proof from 1893.

 Spanish voluntary proof mark 1929-31.

 Royal Arms Factory of Enfield, England trademark on revolver.

 Spanish dimensional inspection mark since 1931.

 German Erfurt Arsenal mark.

 Italian final proof 1923-51.

 Antonio Errasti of Eibar, Spain trademark.

 German rifle proof 1891-1939.

Crowns

 English definitive proof (London 1868-1925).

 East German nitro proof mark.

 Portuguese army crest.

 German nitro proof 1912-39.

 Manufacture Liegeoise d'Armes a Feu of Liege, Belgium trademark.

 French proof on weapons completed but unassembled (St. Etienne).

 Manufacture Liegeoise d'Armes a Feu of Liege, Belgium trademark.

 Spanish final blackpowder proof on shotguns with at least two cocking lugs.

 Mre. Liegeoise d'Armes a Feu of Liege, Belgium trademark.

 English smokeless proof (Birmingham) on rifles of foreign make since 1925.

 Belgian inspector's mark until 1877.

 English smokeless proof mark (Birmingham) since 1904.

Crowns

 French smokeless proof of 1896 (St. Etienne).

 Spanish definitive black-powder proof, ca. 1910.

 French smokeless proof of 1898 (St. Etienne).

 German repair proof 1891-1939.

 Italian first blackpowder proof 1923-51.

 Belgian smokeless proof mark.

 Spanish provisional black-powder proof for shotguns, ca. 1910.

 English reproof mark (Birmingham).

 Italian smokeless preliminary proof 1923-51.

 English reproof mark (London).

 French smokeless proof of 1900 (St. Etienne).

 East German repair proof.

Crowns

 Renkin et Fils of Liege, Belgium trademark.

 Salvador Arostegui of Eibar, Spain.

 Gregorio Bolumburv of Eibar, Spain gripmark on Regina pistol.

 Spanish optional smokeless proof on shotguns.

 English provisional blackpowder proof (Birmingham) since 1856.

 English voluntary special blackpowder proof (Birmingham).

 French blackpowder superior definitive proof (St. Etienne).

 Austro-Hungarian and Hungarian viewing proof mark for Budapest 1891-1928.

 German shotgun proof 1891-1939.

 German Spandau Arsenal mark.

 Danish proof on Sjogren shotguns, ca. 1906.

 French handgun proof (St. Etienne).

Crowns

 French blackpowder double proof (St. Etienne).

 German voluntary proof on guns made before 1891.

 French blackpowder ordinary proof (St. Etienne).

 English inspection mark (London) since 1670.

 Retolaza Hermanos of Eibar, Spain gripmark on Stosel pistols.

 English inspection mark (Birmingham) 1813-1904.

 German 1891 proof for grooved & choked barrels.

 English inspection mark (London) since 1925.

 East German inspection mark.

 Danish arsenal mark of Haerens Vaabenarsenalet.

 German definitive proof 1891-1939.

 Danish arsenal mark of Haerens Vaabenarsenalet.

Crowns

 English definitive proof (Birmingham) 1868-1925.

 Danish function proof.

 San Martin y Cia. of Elgoibar, Spain gripmark on pistols.

 German choked barrel proof 1891-1939.

 Zulaica y Cia., Eibar, Spain gripmark on Royal pistols.

 East German choked barrel mark.

 Dutch military mark on rifles.

 Iranian Acceptance Mark on rifles.

Stars

 Czechoslovakian mark for Weipert 1931-39, and Brno 1946-52.

 Spanish provisional black-powder shotgun proof of 1910.

 Thailand police acceptance mark.

 Italian provisional proof on unfinished barrels since 1951.

 J. M. Marlin of New Haven, Conn. gripmark on revolvers.

 Belgian inspector's mark.

 Czechoslovakian proof used 1919-31 (Prague).

 Astra - Unceta y Cia. trademark.

 Chinese gripmark on Tokarev Pistols.

 Belgian inspector's mark.

 Tula Arsenal, Russia mark on Nagent revolver.

 Tula Arsenal, Russia gripmark on Tokarev pistols.

61

Stars

 Yugoslavian Tokareu Pistol gripmark for guns made at Kragusevac.

 French smokeless proof mark of 1898 (Paris).

 Italian final proof since 1951.

 Italian first blackpowder proof since 1951.

 Hawes Firearms Co. of Los Angeles, Calif. trademark.

 Italian smokeless proof since 1951.

 Belgian inspector's mark.

 Bonifacio Echeverria of Eibar, Spain trademark.

 French smokeless proof mark of 1896 (Paris).

 French smokeless proof mark of 1900 (Paris).

 Bonifacio Echeverria of Eibar, Spain gripmark on Star pistols.

 Bonafacio Echeverria, Eibar, Spain trademark on Star pistols.

Transportation and Buildings

 Bartra y Azpiri of Spain trademark on pistols.

 Webley & Scott of Birmingham, England trademark.

 Ojanguren y Vidosa of Eibar, Spain trademark on pistol.

 Arana y Cia of Eibar, Spain trademark on revolver.

 Isidro Gaztanaga of Eibar, Spain trademark.

Various Inanimate Objects

 Ithaca Gun Co. of Ithaca, N.Y. proof mark.

 Thayer, Robertson & Cary of Norwich, Conn. gripmark on revolver.

 Henrion, Dassy & Heuschen of Liege, Belgium.

 Russian proof mark, Tula, pre-1917.

 Henrion, Dassy & Heuschen of Liege, Belgium.

 Russian proof mark, Tula, pre-1917.

 Thames Arms Co., Norwich, Conn., gripmark on revolvers.

 Spanish Guardia Civil Acceptance Mark.

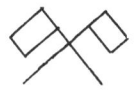 India proof mark 1907-50.

 Belgian inspector's mark for final proof since 1852.

 Spanish final blackpowder proof on underlever shotguns, 1910-29 (Eibar)

 India provisional proof since 1957.

Geometric Designs

 Gerstenberger u. Eberwein of Gussenstadt, West Germany gripmark on revolvers.

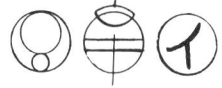 Nagoya Arsenal, Japan 1941-43 on Nambu pistols.

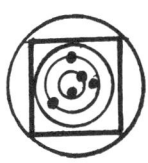 Harrington & Richardson of Gardner, Mass. gripmark on revolvers.

 Nagoya Arsenal, Japan 1941-43.

 Stoeger Industries of South Hackensack, N. J. trademark.

 Japanese Mukden Arsenal, Manchuria mark on rifles.

 Japanese Kokura Arsenal mark 1928-35.

 Toriimatsu Factory of Nagoya Arsenal, Japan mark.

 Japanese Nagoya Arsenal mark 1927-32.

 Spanish definitive blackpowder proof on shotguns 1929-31.

 Nagoya Arsenal, Japan 1935-41 on Nambu pistols.

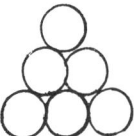 Spanish definitive proof mark on blackpowder double shotguns 1923-25.

 Nagoya Arsenal, Japan 1943-45.

 Sweden definitive proof on Carl Gustav rifles.

Geometric Designs

 Tula Weapons Factory, Tula, Russia, Commercial mark on Korovin pistols.

 Russian trademark on Makarov pistols.

 Russian Tula proof mark.

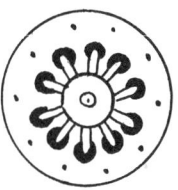 Meriden Firearms Co. of Conn. gripmark on revolvers.

 Finland proof mark before 1966.

 Maltby-Henley Co. of New York City gripmark on revolvers.

 Portuguese military acceptance mark.

 Industria Armi Galesi of Brescia, Italy gripmark on Model 9 pistol.

 Steyr Daimler - Puch of Steyr, Austria trademark.

 Finland proof mark since 1966.

 Carl Walther Waffenfabrik, Ulm, West Germany gripmark on Mod TP pistol.

 Merwin, Hulbert & Co. of N.Y.C. gripmark on revolvers.

Geometric Designs

 Henry M. Kolb of Philadelphia, Pa. gripmark.

 Retolaza Hermanos of Eibar, Spain gripmark on "Velobrom" revolver.

 Harrington & Richardson of Worcester, Mass. gripmark on revolver.

 Francisco Arizmendi of Eibar, Spain trademark on handguns.

 J. C. Higgins (Sears, Roebuck) gripmark.

 Spanish blackpowder provisional proof on shotguns since 1910.

 Merwin, Hulbert & Co. of N.Y.C. gripmark on revolvers.

 Simson & Co. of Suhl, Germany trademark on pistols.

 Marlin Firearms Co. of New Haven, Conn. gripmark on revolvers.

 Harrington & Richardson of Gardner, Mass. gripmark on revolvers.

Geometric Designs

 Kirikale Tufek Fb. of Kirikale, Turkey gripmark.

 Swiss rejection mark.

 Alois Tomiska of Pilsen, Czechoslovakia gripmark on Fox pistol.

 Finland examiner's mark.

 Finland examiner's mark.

 Hopkins & Allen of Norwich, Conn. gripmark on revolvers.

 Mre. de Machines du Haut Rhin of Mulhouse-Bourtzwiller, France trademark.

 Lithuanian Coat of Arms.

 Tallares Armas Livianas Argentinas of Punta Alta, Argentina.

 Russian Izhevsk proof mark.

 Finland tenacity test mark.

Geometric Designs

 Siamese crest.

 Austro-Hungarian and Hungarian 1st proof for Budapest 1891-1928.

 French preliminary black-powder proof (Paris).

 Gaspar Arizaga of Eibar, Spain cartridge indicator on Pinkerton .25 pistol grip.

 Swiss rejection mark.

 Hungarian provisional proof for unfinished barrels 1929-71.

 Hungarian provisional and voluntary proof since 1971.

Birds

 German proof for Flobert rifles 1939-45.

 German voluntary proof 1939-45.

 Miroku Firearms Mfg. Co. Ltd. of Kochi, Japan trademark on shotguns.

 West German voluntary proof.

 Polish mark on Radom pistols.

 Fabryka Bronn Radom of Radom, Poland trademark on rifles.

 East German definitive proof.

 West German flobert rifle proof.

 German army acceptance mark.

 West German proof, Cologne.

 German Nazi police procurement mark.

 West German repair proof.

Birds

 German re-proof mark 1939-45.

 German definitive nitro proof 1939-45.

 German Nazi police procurement mark.

 West German definitive nitro proof.

 German Nazi naval acceptance mark.

 German definitive blackpowder proof 1939-45.

 German Weimar naval acceptance mark.

 West German definitive blackpowder proof.

 West German provisional proof.

 Austro-Hungarian Prague proof mark used 1891-99.

 German provisional blackpowder proof 1939-45.

 German Waffen Amt military acceptance mark.

Birds

 German Nazi party mark (NSKK) on Walther pistols.

 U.S. Arms Corp. of Riverhead, N.Y. trademark.

 German Nazi military proof.

 Francisco Arizmendi of Eibar, Spain trademark on pistols.

 Francisco Arizmendi of Eibar, Spain on "Singer" pistol.

 Hopkins & Allen trademark.

 German Luftwaffe Mark.

 High Standard Mfg. Co. of New Haven, Conn. trademark.

 Iver Johnson of Fitchburg, Mass. gripmark on revolvers.

 Tiroler Maschinenbau u. Hoizindustrie of Kufstein, Tirol, Austria trademark.

 Golden Eagle Firearms (Nikko) trademark on shotguns.

 Apaoloza Hermanos of Zumoraaga, Spain trademark.

Birds

 Alder Waffenwerke of Zella St. Blasil, Germany trademark on pistol.

 Fab. d'Armes Jannsen et Fils of Liege, Belgium trademark.

 Republic of China provisional proof on police pistols since 1964.

 Ithaca Gun Co. trademark on buttplates.

 U. S. Springfield Armory inspector's mark on M1911 pistols.

 Gaspar Arizaga of Eibar, Spain trademark on pistols.

 Gebruder Merkel of Suhl, Germany trademark on rifles and shotguns.

 Spesco of Atlanta, Ga. gripmark on pistols.

 Mre. Liegeoise d'Armes a Feu of Liege, Belgium trademark.

 Sturm, Ruger & Co. of Southport, Conn. trademark on pistols and revolvers.

 Fab d'Armes Jannsen et Fils of Liege, Belgium trademark.

 Sturm, Ruger & Co. of Southport, Conn. trademark.

73

Hearts

 Stoeger Arms Corp. of N.Y. trademark.

 Iver Johnson gripmark on revolvers.

 Gabilondo y Cia. gripmark on Plus Ultra pistol.

 Iver Johnson of Fitchburg, Mass. trademark.

 Austro-Hungarian and Austrian viewing proof mark. 1 signifies Ferlach, 2 is Prague, 3 is Weipert, and 4 is Vienna.

Hearts

 East India Company (English) proof mark.

 East India Company (English) proof mark.

Lions

 Relay Products (Pty.) Ltd. of Johannesburg, South Africa trademark on Mamba pistols.

 Dansk Industri Syndikat, Companie Madsen of Copenhagen, Denmark, trademark on machine guns.

 Harrington & Richardson of Worcester, Mass. trademark.

 Mre. d'Armes des Pyrenees on Hendaye, France trademark on pistols.

 Czechoslovakian proof for Prague since 1931.

 Finland definitive smokeless proof mark.

 West German proof, Berlin.

 Finland definitive smokeless proof.

 Spanish definitive proof on handguns 1923-29.

 Retolaza Hermanos of Eibar, Spain gripmark.

 Belgian mark on guns sent from Liege to be proofed at a foreign proof house.

 Lee E. Jurras of Shelbyville, Indiana trademark.

Lions

 Italian provisional proof mark 1923-51 (Brescia).

 Aguirre y Aranzabal of Eibar, Spain trademark on shotguns and rifles.

 Industria Armi Galesi of Brescia, Italy gripmark on pistols.

 India definitive black-powder proof since 1957.

 Czechoslovakian 5th proof since 1931.

 English provisional proof since about 1868 (London).

 Czechoslovakian mark for Brno 1946-52.

 English provisional proof on foreign arms since 1925 (London).

 Czechoslovakian proof used 1919-31 (Weipert).

 Belgian voluntary proof mark for smokeless powder since 1891.

Lions

 Echave y Arizmendi of Eibar, Spain trademark.

 India definitive nitro proof since 1957.

 Harrington & Richardson of Gardner, Mass. trademark.

 Belgian proof mark on rifled barrels since 1924.

 Castelli of Brescia, Italy trademark on Italian Service Revolvers.

 India proof mark since 1950.

 L.E.S. of Slokie, Ill. trademark on pistols.

 India re-proof mark since 1957.

 English voluntary proof (London for blackpowder).

 India special definitive proof since 1957.

 English smokeless proof (London) on rifles of foreign make since 1925.

 English final proof mark used 1868-1925 (London).

Dogs

 Hopkins & Allen of Norwich, Conn. gripmark on revolvers.

 Burgess Gun Co. trademark found on buttplates.

 Iver Johnson of Fitchburg, Mass. gripmark on revolvers.

 Parker Bros. of Meriden, Conn. trademark on buttplates.

 Iver Johnson of Fitchburg, Mass. gripmark on Bulldog revolvers.

 Parker Bros. of Meriden, Conn. trademark on buttplates.

 Forehand & Wadsworth of Worcester, Mass. trademark on revolvers.

 L. C. Smith Gun Co. of Syracuse, N.Y. trademark on buttplates.

Horses

 Colt Pt. F. A. Co. of Hartford, Conn. gripmark on revolvers.

 Ernesto Breda of Milan, Italy trademark.

 Colt Pt. F. A. Co. of Hartford, Conn. trademark.

 Colt's Pt. F. A. Mfg. Co. of Hartford, Conn. trademark.

 Retolaza Hermanos of Eibar, Spain gripmark on Stosel pistol.

 Hebsacher Gesellschaft of West Germany trademark used on pistols made in Budapest, Hungary.

 Colt Pt. F. A. Co. of Hartford, Conn. gripmark on pistols.

 Marlin Firearms Co. of New Haven, Conn. trademark.

 Armalite, Inc. of Costa Mesa, Calif. trademark.

 Zulaica y Cia of Eibar, Spain gripmark on pistols.

Bears

 Kodiak trademark on rifles.

 Reising Mfg. Corp. of New York City gripmark on pistols.

 Fiala Arms & Eqpt. Co. of New Haven, Conn. trademark on pistols.

Insects

 Fab. d'Armes Jannsen et Fils of Liege, Belgium trademark.

 Triple-S Development Co., Wickliffe, Ohio trademark on rifles.

Deer

 Liege United Arms Co. of Liege, Belgium trademark on revolver.

 Julien Doyen Fab. d'Armes of Herstal, Belgium trademark on shotguns.

 West German mark of the Ulm proof house.

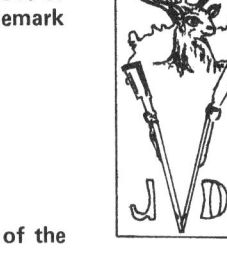 Browning Arms Co. of Morgan, Utah trademark.

 Etab. Radarm Fabrique d'Armes of Liege, Belgium trademark on shotguns.

 G. C. Dornheim of Suhl, Germany.

Buffalo

 Cody Mfg. Co. of Springfield, Mass. trademark on Thunderbird pistols.

 Gabilondo y Cia. of Elgoibar, Spain gripmark on Buffalo pistol.

 Rocky Mountain Arms Corp. of Salt Lake City, Utah trademark.

 Sharps Arms Co. of Salt Lake City, Utah trademark.

Various Animals

 Garate, Anitua y Cia., of Eibar, Spain gripmark on Cesar and Secours pistols.

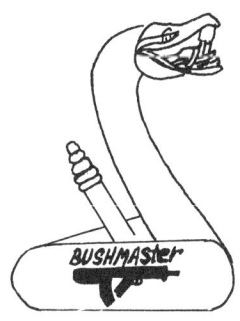 Gwinn Arms Corp. of Winston-Salem, N.C. trademark.

 Tiroler Waffenfabrik Peterlongo of Innsbruck, Austria trademark.

 Garate, Anitua y Cia of Eibar, Spain trademark on "La Lira" pistols.

 E. Mayor of Geneva, Switzerland trademark on pistols.

 Victor Sarasqueta of Spain trademark on shotguns.

 Garate, Anitua y Cia of Eibar, Spain trademark on "Express" pistol.

 Echave y Arizmendi of Eibar, Spain trademark on pistols.

Humans

Hopkins and Allen of Norwich, Conn. trademark on revolvers.

J.P. Sauer u. Sohn of Suhl, Germany gripmark.

Friederich Pickert of Zella-Mehlis, Germany trademark.

Schutzmerke

Frommer of Budapest, Hungary trademark on Liliput pistol.

Classic Arms Ltd. of Palmer, Mass. trademark.

Savage Arms Corp. of Westfield, Mass. trademark.

J. P. Sauer & Sohn of West Germany trademark.

J. P. Sauer & Sohn of West Germany trademark.

Gabilondo y Cia of Spain, trademark on Tauler pistols.

Fab. d'Armes Jannsen et Fils of Liege, Belgium trademark.

Soc. Anonyme des Fabriques d'Armes Reunies of Liege, Belgium gripmark on Dictator pistol.

Humans

Arizmendi y Goenaga on Eibar, Spain trademark on pistols.

A. Aldazabal of Eibar, Spain trademark.

Anciens Etablissments Pieper of Herstal, Belgium trademark.

Fabrique d'Armes Unies de Liege of Belgium, trademark on sporting arms.

Anciens Etablissments Pieper trademark on shotguns.

Luigi Franchi of Brescia, Italy trademark on shotguns.

Larranaga y Elartza of Eibar, Spain gripmark on Jubala pistol.

VEB Fahrzeug u. Jagdwaffenwerk Ernst Thalmann of Suhl, East Germany trademark.

Mre. d'Armes Le Page of Liege, Beligum.

Ojanguren y Vidosa of Eibar, Spain trademark on pistols.

Gabilondo y Cia of Elgoibar, Spain trademark.

Humans

 Manifattura Armi Perazzi of Brescia, Italy trademark on shotguns.

 Savage Arms Corp. gripmark on Model 1917 pistol.

 Savage Arms Corp. of Westfield, Mass. gripmark on pistols.

 C. H. Masquelier of Liege, Belgium trademark on shotguns.

 Tauler of Madrid, Spain trademark on pistols made for them by Gabilondo y Cia.

 English smokeless proof for foreign rifles since 1925 (London).

 Universal Firearms Corp. of Hialeah, Fla. trademark.

 Mre. d'Armes des Pyrenees of Hendaye, France trademark on pistols.

 Mre. d'Armes des Pyrenees of Hendaye, France trademark on pistols.

 V. Charles Schilling of Gaggenau, Germany trademark on Bergmann pistols.

 Mre. d'Armes des Pyrenees of Hendaye, France.

 Webley & Scott of Birmingham, England trademark.

Plants

 Gregorio Bolumburu of Eibar, Spain gripmark.

 Albrecht Kind of Berlin-Nurnberg, Germany trademark.

 Eulogio Arostegui, Eibar, Spain gripmark on Azul pistol.

 Japanese crest.

 Hammerli of Lenzburg, Switzerland, trademark.

 "J. C. Higgins" (Sears, Roebuck) trademark used on High Standard revolver.

 Trejo, Zacatlan, Mexico gripmark on pistols.

 Fabrique Nationale of Herstal, Belgium, trademark.

 West German Eckernforde proof house mark since 1952.

 Tallares Armas Livians Argentinas of Punta Alta, Argentina trademark.

 Albrecht Kind of Berlin-Nurnberg, Germany trademark.

Plants

 L. Bergeron of St. Etienne, France gripmark on Le Steph pistol.

 Trejo, Zacatcan, Mexico trademark on pistols.

 L. Gasser of Vienna, Austria trademark on revolvers.

Crests

 Czechoslovakian crest.

 Portuguese crest.

 Persian crest on Mauser pistols.

 Czechoslovakian coat of arms.

 Glisenti gripmark on Italian service pistols.

 Bolivian crest.

 Chilean coat of arms.

 Yugoslavian crest.

 U. S. crest.

 Bulgarian crest.

Crests

 Ethiopian crest.

 Swiss police crest.

 Hungarian crest.

 Argentinian crest

 J. L. Galef & Son of N.Y.C. trademark.

 Bulgarian crest.

 Persian coat of arms.

 Italian provisional proof since 1951 (Brescia).

 Italian provisional proof (Gardone) 1930-51.

 Bulgarian coat of arms.

 Spanish admission proof for Eibar since 1931.

Crests

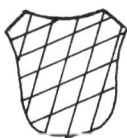 West German proof, Munich.

 Spanish definitive proof for military style rifles 1923-25.

 Bliss & Goodyear of New Haven, Conn. gripmark on revolvers.

 Winslow Arms Co. of Osprey, Fla. trademark on rifles.

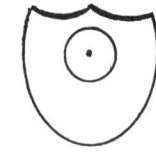 Spanish definitive proof on non-automatic rifled handguns since 1931.

 Yugoslavian crest used by Mikhailovich.

 Spanish admission mark for Barcelona 1929-31.

 Russian Izhevsk proof mark.

 West German proof at Eckernforde.

 Armsport, Inc. of Miami, Fla. trademark on imported guns.

 Spanish definitive proof of nonautomatic handguns 1923-29.

Crests

 Austro-Hungarian and Austrian 2nd proof for Vienna since 1891.

 French superior definitive blackpowder proof (Paris).

 Harrington & Richardson of Worcester, Mass. gripmark on revolver.

 Spanish admission mark (Eibar) 1929-31.

 Harrington & Richardson of Gardner, Mass. gripmark on revolvers.

 Italian provisional proof since 1951 (Gardone).

 Spanish definitive proof of nonautomatic handguns 1923-29.

 Adolph Frank Export Co. of Hamburg, Germany trademark.

 Austro-Hungarian and Czechoslovakian 2nd proof for Weipert 1891-1931.

 Adolph Frank Export Co. of Hamburg, Germany trademark.

 French ordinary definitive blackpowder proof (Paris).

 Hungarian definitive blackpowder proof since 1929.

Crests

 Spanish optional smokeless proof on shotguns since 1931.

 Forehand & Wadsworth of Worcester, Mass. gripmark on revolvers.

 B.S.A. of Birmingham, England trademark.

 Herter's Inc. of Waseca, Minn. trademark.

 Congolese marking.

 Hijos de Jose Aldazabal of Eibar, Spain trademark.

 Armi Famars trademark on shotguns.

 East German standard proof.

 Spanish La Caruna Arsenal mark.

 Hungarian definitive nitro proof since 1929.

 Mexican crest.

Crests

 East German definitive smokeless proof.

 Hungarian re-proof mark since 1971.

 Hungarian definitive nitro proof since 1971.

 East German repair proof.

 Norrahammer trademark on rifles.

 East German definitive blackpowder proof.

 Paraguayan coat of arms.

 East German re-enforced proof.

 Peruvian crest.

 Greek coat of arms.

 Peruvian crest.

 Guatemalan crest.

NAMES AND CODES

A

A.A. — Tradename of Azanza y Arrizabalaga.

aaa — WW-II German ordnance code assigned to Waffenfabrik Brunn AG, Prague, Czechoslovakia.

A.A.A. — Abbreviation and trade name used by A. Aldazabal of Eibar Spain.

aac — WW-II German ordnance code assigned to Mannesman-Rohrenwerke, Komotau, Germany.

aaj — WW-II German ordnance code assigned to Obenhutten, Vereinigte Oberschlesische Huttenwerke AG.

aak — WW-II German ordnance code assigned to Waffenwerke Brunn AG, Prague, Czechoslovakia, Wrsoviace plant.

aan — WW-II German ordnance code assigned to Mitteldeutsche Mettalwarenfabrik, Erich Frank, Glauchau, Germany.

aar — WW-II German ordnance code assigned to Geba-Munitions und Waffenfabrik, Breslau, Czechoslovakia.

aaw — WW-II German ordnance code assigned to Mettalwarenfabrik Gebr. Schmidt, Idar-Oberstein, Germany.

abb — WW-II German ordnance code assigned to Friedrichsthaler Eisenwerk, Jennewein & Gapp, Friedrichsthal, Germany.

abc — WW-II German ordnance code assigned to Deutsche Metallwerke, Weinstrabe, Germany.

ABERCROMBIE & FITCH — Distributors and importers formerly based in N.Y.C. In 1978 purchased by Houston based sporting goods chain of Oshman's, with A. & F. stores to be located in Beverly Hills, Calif. and Dallas, Tex.

abh — WW-II German ordnance code assigned to Koch & Sohne, Frankental-Plomerscheim.

ac — WW-II German ordnance code assigned to Carl Walther, Zella-Mehlis, Germany.

ACCURATE ACE — Tradename on derringers imported by Hy Hunter of Burbank, Calif., ca. 1960.

ACHA, DOMINGO Y CIA. — Manufacturer of handguns in Ermua, Spain about 1927-37.

ACIER COMPRIME — Tradename on revolvers from Apaolozo Hermanos.

ACKLEY, P.O., INC. — Custom rifle maker and importer of rifle actions made for them in Japan, ca. 1969.

ACME — Tradename on spur trigger revolvers made by Hopkins & Allen and sold by Merwin, Hulbert & Co., ca. 1885.

ACME ARMS — Tradename used by J. Stevens Arms Co., ca. 1880.

ACME HAMMERLESS — Tradename used by Hulbert Bros. on revolvers made by Hopkins & Allen, ca. 1893.

ACRA — Tradename used by Reinhart Fajen on Santa Barbara rifles, ca. 1970.

ACTION — Tradename of Modesto Santos on pistols.

ad — WW-II German ordnance code assigned to Patronen, Zundhutchen und Metallwarenfabrik AG (Sellier & Bellot)

ADAMS PATENT SMALL ARMS CO. — London, England 1864-92. Manufacturer of John Adams designed firearms.

ADAMY GEBR. — Sporting arms makers in Suhl, Germany, about 1921-39.

adc — WW-II German ordnance code assigned to William Prym, Stollberg, Germany.

ADIRONDACK ARMS CO. — Made lever action rifles under the Robinson patent in Plattsburg, N.Y. from 1870 until 1874 when they were absorbed by Winchester.

ADLER — Tradename of Adlerwaffenwerke.

ADLERWAFFENWERKE — Zella St. Blasii, Germany 1904 to 1906. Distributor of the Adler pistol, which was made for them by Engelbrecht & Wolff.

aek — WW-II German ordnance code assigned to F. Dusek Waffenerzeugung, Oppeln, Czechoslovakia.

A.E.P. — Abbreviation and tradename of Anciens Etablissmants Pieper.

AETNA — Tradename on spur trigger revolvers made by Harrington & Richardson, ca. 1876.

AETNA ARMS CO. — Manufactured tip-up revolvers in New York City 1880-90.

AF — Abbreviation for August Francotte & Co.

A & F — Abbreviation for Abercrombie & Fitch.

afb — WW-II German ordnance code assigned to Metabu, Werk Closs, Rauch & Schnitzler, Nurtingen, Germany.

AFRICAN MAGNUM — Tradename used by Tyrol Sporting Arms Co. of St. Albans, Vt. on imported rifles.

AFRO — INDIA — Tradename on double rifles made by Sarasqueta for A.F. Stoeger.

A.F.S. — Abbreviation for A.F. Stoeger, Importers in New York City, and now in Hackensack, New Jersey.

afu — WW-II German ordnance code assigned to August Winkhaus, Munster, Germany.

A. G. — Abbreviation of Armand Gavage (Fab. d'Armes de Guerre Haute Precision Armand Gavage).

AGAWAM ARMS — Manufacturer of rifles in Agawam, Mass., ca. 1970.

AGUIRRE Y ARANZABAL — see A Y A.

AGURU — Tradename of Erquiaga Muguruza.

AJAX ARMY — Tradename on revolvers sold by E.C. Meacham Co., ca. 1880.

ajf — WW-II German ordnance code assigned to Junker & Ruh AG, Karlsruhe, Germany.

ajn — WW-II German ordnance code assigned to Union Sprengstoff u. Zundmittlewerke, Alt-Berum, Germany.

ak — WW-II German ordnance code assigned to Munitionsfabriken, Vlasim, Czechoslovakia (Sellier & Bellot).

AKAH — Tradename of dealer Albrecht Kind of Berlin-Nürnberg, Germany, ca. 1920.

akp — WW-II German ordnance code assigned to Deutsche Rohrenwerke, Ponsgen plant, Dusseldorf, Germany.

al — WW-II German ordnance code assigned to Deutsche Leucht u. Signalwerke, Berlin, Germany.

ALAMO — Tradename on revolvers used by A.F. Stoeger on guns from West Germany.

ALASKA — Tradename used by Hood Firearms Co., ca. 1875.

ALDAZABAL — Tradename used by Hijos de Jose Aldazabal.

ALDAZABAL Y LETURIONDO — Pistol maker in Eibar, Spain, ca. 1915.

ALERT — Tradename on revolvers from Hood Firearms Co., ca. 1875.

ALEXIA — Tradename used by Hopkins & Allen, ca. 1880.

ALEXIS — Tradename used by Turner & Ross Co., Boston, Mass. on revolvers made by Hood Firearms Co., ca. 1875.

ALFA — Tradename used by Adolf Frank of Hamburg, Germany, a distributor of all types of arms around 1900 (Germany).

ALFA — Tradename of Armero Especialistas Reunidas (Spain).

ALKAR — Tradename of Alkartasuna Fab. de Armas.

ALKARTASUNA FABRICA DE ARMAS, A.A. — Guernica, Spain 1917 to about 1922. Manufactured under license from Gabilondo y Cia. the "Ruby" type pistol, which was used as a secondary French military arm. Brand name was "Alkar."

ALLEN — Tradename used by McKeown's Guns on Italian shotguns, ca. 1970.

ALLEN — Tradename on revolvers made by Hopkins & Allen, ca. 1880.

ALLEN DERRINGER — Model designation used by Ethan Allen & Co., ca. 1870.

ALLIES — Tradename used by Domingo Acha.

ALLIES — Tradename of Berasaluze Areitio-Arutena y Cia., Elbar, Spain, ca. 1920 on pistols.

ALPINE INDUSTRIES — Makers of M-1 carbines in Los Angeles, Calif. from 1962 to 1965.

am — WW-II German ordnance code assigned to Otto Eberhardt Patronenfabrik, Hirtenberg, Austria (Gustloff Co.).

AM — Abbreviation on Italian military arms meaning Aeronautica Militare (Air Force).

A & M RIFLE CO. — Abbreviation for Atkinson & Marquart of Prescott, Ariz. from about 1960 to the early 1970's.

AMERICA — Tradename on double action revolvers made by Norwich Falls Pistol Co., ca. 1880.

AMERICA — Tradename used on spur trigger revolvers from Bliss & Goodyear, ca. 1878.

AMERICAN — Tradename on double action revolvers from Harrington & Richardson.

AMERICAN ARMS CO. — Manufacturers of shotguns and two shot Wheeler patent derringers. In Boston, Mass. from 1873 to 93, in Milwaukee, Wisc. from 1893 until they were purchased by Marlin Firearms Co. in 1901.

AMERICAN BARLOCK WONDER — Tradename used by Sears, Roebuck & Co. on shotguns made by Crescent Firearms Co.

AMERICAN BOY — Tradename used by Townley Hdw. Co. on revolvers made by Bliss & Goodyear, ca. 1878.

AMERICAN BULLDOG — Tradename used on revolvers from Johnson, Bye & Co., 1882 to about 1900.

AMERICAN DOUBLE ACTION — Tradename on revolvers made by Harrington & Richardson, ca. 1900.

AMERICAN EAGLE — Tradename used by Hopkins & Allen on revolvers, ca. 1880.

AMERICAN FIREARMS MFG. CO. — Pistol maker in San Antonio, Tex. from 1966-74.

AMERICAN GUN CO. — Tradename of H. & D. Folsom Co. on shotguns made by Crescent Firearms Co.

AMERICAN INTERNATIONAL — Importers in Salt Lake City, Utah of .22 caliber machine guns and carbines from Austria.

AMERICAN STANDARD TOOL CO. — Manufacturers of tip-up revolvers in Newark, N.J., ca. 1865-70.

AMERICAN WEAPONS CORP. — Company name used by Hy Hunter, ca. 1955.

AMERICUS — Tradename of revolvers made by Hopkins & Allen, ca. 1880.

amn — WW-II German ordnance code assigned to Mauser-Werke, Neuwied plant.

amo — WW-II German ordnance code assigned to Mauser-Werke, Waldeck-Kassel plant.

amp — WW-II German ordnance code assigned to Dortmund Hoerder Huttenverein, Dortmund, Germany.

AMT — Abbreviation for Arcadia Machine & Tool Co., best known for their stainless steel pistols since 1976 in Arcadia, Calif.

an — WW-II German ordnance code assigned to Beutemuller & Co. GmbH, Mettallwarenfabrik, Bretten-Baden, Germany.

ANCIENS ETABLISSMENTS PIEPER — Successor to Henry Pieper, and synonymous with Nicolas Pieper. From 1907 to 1939, mainly known for their pistols, especially the "Bayard" line.

ANCION-MARX FAB. D'ARMES — Manufacturer of sporting arms in Liege, Belgium 1934-39.

and — WW-II German Ordnance code assigned to Magdeburger Pumpenfabrik, Otterburg & Co., Magdeburg, Germany.

anj — WW-II German code assigned to Kienzle-Uhrenfabrik, Lomotau, Germany.

ANSCHUTZ, BRUNO — Manufacturer of sporting arms in Zella-Mehlis, Germany 1919-26.

ANSCHUTZ, J.G. — Sporting arms manufacturer, especially known for target rifles. Established 1922 and operated until 1938 in Zella-Mehlis, Germany. After the war resumed production in Ulm, West Germany. Imported into the U.S. by Savage Arms Corp. and sometimes called "Savage/Anschutz."

ANSCHUTZ, UDO — Manufacturer of sporting arms in Zella-Mehlis, Germany 1927-39, best known for his "Free-Pistols."

anx — WW-II German ordnance code assigned to Konigs-Laura-Hutte, Konigshutte, Germany.

anz — WW-II German ordnance code assigned to Maschinen u. Armaturenfabrik, Div. of Polte, Magdeburg-Backau, Germany (L. Strube).

A.O.A. — Abbreviation for Asahi Okuma Arms Co., Ltd., current ammunition manufacturers in Japan on guns made by Howa.

ap — WW-II German ordnance code assigned to Gustloff-Werke, Wuppertal plant, Ronsdorf, Germany, and to Otto Eberhardt, Patronenfabrik, Hirtenberg, Germany.

APACHE — Tradename of Ojanguren y Vidosa on pistols.

APACHE — Tradename on revolvers from Fab. de Armas Garantazadas (Spain).

APACHE — Tradename used by Jana International on revolvers imported from Germany, ca. 1976.

APAOLOZO HERMANOS — Revolver makers in Zumorraga, Spain.

apc — WW-II German ordnance code assigned to Continental Caoutchouc Co., Hannover, Germany.

aqe — WW-II German ordnance code assigned to Deutsche Kabelwerke, Berlin, Germany.

aqx — WW-II German ordnance code assigned to Rheinmetall-Borsig, Tegel plant.

ar — German WW-II ordnance code assigned to Mauser-Werke, Berlin-Borsigwalde.

A & R SALES CO. — Manufacturer of M1911 .45 frames and military rifle receivers, dealer of surplus military gun parts, since 1969 in South El Monte, Calif.

ARANA Y CIA. — Manufacturer of revolvers in Eibar, Spain.

arb — German WW-II ordnance code assigned to Vereinigte Oberschlesige Huttenwerke, Andreashutte, Germany.

ARICO — Tradename used by Nicolas Pieper.

ARISTOCRAT — Tradename on revolvers from Hopkins & Allen for Suplee Biddle Hardware, ca. 1880.

ARISTOCRAT — Tradename used by J. Stevens Arms Co. on shotguns.

ARIZAGA — Tradename of Gaspar Ariziba of Eibar, Spain on pistols, ca. 1920.

ARIZMENDI, FRANCISCO — See Arizmendi y Goenaga.

ARIZMENDI Y GOENAGA — From 1886 to 1914 in Eibar, Spain. In 1914 the name was changed to Francisco Arizmendi. The earlier company was best known for their revolvers, while after 1914 the emphasis was changed to pistols, and they were produced under many tradenames.

ARMALITE, INC. — Costa Mesa, Calif. from about 1959, division of Fairchild. Developed the Stoner system of military arms, and also makes sporting arms. Tradename and model designation is "AR." Present production is subcontracted by Sterling Armament Co. Ltd. License for the AR-7 Explorer has been given to Charter Arms, and for the AR-15 and M-16 to Colt.

ARMAS TREJO, A.A. — Manufacturers of semi, and full automatic pistols in Zacatlan, Mexico.

ARMERO ESPECIALISTAS REUNIDOS — Revolver makers in Eibar, Spain.

ARMI FAMARS — Current manufacturer of sporting arms in Brescia, Italy.

ARMI GALESI — See Industria Armi Galesi.

ARMI JAGER — Current manufacturer of sporting arms in Turin, Italy.

ARMINIUS —Tradename of Friederich Pickert, pre-WW-II (Germany).

ARMINIUS — Postwar brandname used by Herman Weirauch Sportwaffenfabrik, West Germany on revolvers. Marketed by several U.S. distributors until around 1969. Now made in the U.S. by F.I.E.

ARMINIUS — Tradename of Gregorio Bolumburu (Spain).

ARMSPORT — Importers, Miami, Fla.

AROSTIGUI, EULOGIO — Revolver maker in Eibar, Spain.

AROSTIGUI, SALVADOR — Revolver maker in Eibar, Spain.

ARRIOLA HERMANOS — Revolver makers in Eibar, Spain.

ARTISTIC ARMS, INC. — Current manufacturer of reproduction Sharp's rifles in Hoagland, Indiana since about 1971.

asb — WW-II German ordnance code assigned to Deutsche Waffen u. Munitionsfabriken, Berlin, Germany.

asr — WW-II German ordnance code assigned to HAK Hanseatisches-Kettenwerke, Hamburg, Germany.

A.S.T. — Abbreviation for American Standard Tool Co.

ASTORIA — Tradename on rifles made by Berlin-Suhler Waffen u. Fahrzengwerke in pre-WW-II Germany.

ASTRA — Tradename of Astra-Unceta y Cia. S.A. The company was formed under the name Pedro Unceta y Juan Esperanza in 1908 in Eibar, Spain. In 1913 the company moved to Guernica, Spain, and sometime between then and 1926 the name was reversed to Esperanza y Unceta. In 1926 the name was changed to Unceta y Cia., and in 1953 was changed to its current form Astra-Unceta y Cia. The firm makes contract military arms, and a variety of arms for the commercial market.

asx — WW-II German ordnance code

assigned to Hosch AG, Dortmund plant, Dortmund, Germany.

at — WW-II German ordnance code assigned to Klockner-Werke, Division of Haspner Eisen u. Stahlwerk.

atb — WW-II German ordnance code assigned to Hydrometer AG, Breslau, Czechoslovakia.

ATC — Tradename and abbreviation for Armas de Tiro y Caza, S.A.

ATCSA — Tradename and abbreviation for Armas de Tiro y Caza, S.A.

ATIS SpA — Current firearms manufacturers in Ponte S. Marco, Italy.

ATKINSON & MARQUART RIFLE CO. — See A & M Rifle Co.

atl — WW-II German ordnance code assigned to Klockner-Humbold-Deutz, Ulm, Germany.

ATLAS — Tradename of Domingo Acha.

ATLAS — Tradename of Tomas de Urizar y Cia.

ATLAS ARMS — Importers in Chicago, Ill. from the early 1960's. Moved to Niles, Ill. about 1970, and out of business about 1972.

atr — WW-II German ordnance code assigned to Langbein-Pfannhauser-Werke AG, Leipzig, Germany.

atw — WW-II German ordnance code assigned to Mannesman-Rohrenwerke AG, Witten plant, Ruhr, Germany.

aty — WW-II German ordnance code assigned to Machinenfabrik fur Massenpackung, Lubeck-Schlutrup, Germany.

au — WW-II German ordnance code assigned to Gute-Hoffnungshutte Oberhausen, Sterkrade plant, Germany.

AUBREY, A.J. — Tradename of Sears, Roebuck & Co. on firearms made by Meriden Arms Co.

auc — WW-II German ordnance code assigned to Mauser-Werke AG, Cologne-Ehrenfeld, Germany.

AUDAX — Tradename of Mre. d'Armes des Pyrenees.

auf — WW-II German ordnance code assigned to Metall, Guss, u. Presswerk, Nurnberg, Germany (H. Diehl).

aure — WW-II German ordnance code assigned to Metall u. Eisen GmbH, Nurnberg, Germany.

AUTO AND BURGLAR GUN — Tradename used on shotgun pistols made by Ithaca Gun Co.

AUTOGARDE — Tradename of Soc. Francaise des Munitions.

AUTOMATIC — Tradename of Mre. d'Armes a Feu.

AUTOMATIC DERRINGER — Tradename used by Hy Hunter on 2-shot pistols made in West Germany by Gerstenberger & Eberwein.

AUTOMATIC HAMMERLESS — Tradename used on double action hammerless revolvers by Iver Johnson.

AUTOMATICO VB — Tradename used by Bernardelli on automatic shotguns.

AUTOMATIQUE FRANCAISE — Tradename of Soc. Francaise d'Armes Automatiques.

AUTO — ORDNANCE CORP. Developers of the Thompson submachine gun, in New York City, ca. 1920.

AUTO-POINTER — Tradename used on shotguns imported by Sloan's and made by Yamamoto Mfg. Co.

AUTO-STAND — Tradname on pistols made by Mre. d'Armes des Pyrenees for Manufrance.

auu — WW-II German ordnance code assigned to Patronenhulsen u. Metallwarenfabrik AG, Rikycany plant, Pilsen, Czechoslovakia.

aux — WW-II German ordnance code assigned to Polte-Werk, Magdeburg, Germany.

auy — WW-II German ordnance code assigned to Polte-Werk, Grunberg, Germany.

auz — WW-II German ordnance code assigned to Polte-Werk, Arnstadt, Germany.

av — WW-II German ordnance code assigned to Adam Gerhard Moterenwerke, Oskau Friedrichsdorf, Sudeten, Germany.

AVION — Tradename of Bartra y Azpiri.

avk — WW-II German ordnance code assigned to Ruhrstahl AG, Brackwede-Beilefeld, Germany.

avm — WW-II German ordnance code assigned to Rheinhutte GmbH, Wiesbaden, Germany (Beck & Co.).

avt — WW-II German ordnance code assigned to Silva-Metallwerke, Division of Polte, Genthin, Germany.

awl — WW-II German ordnance code assigned to Union-Gesellschaft fur Metallindustrie, Werl plant, Frondenberg, Ruhr, Germany.

awt — WW-II German ordnance code assigned to Wurttembergische Metallwarenfabrik AG, Geislingen, Germany.

A.W.Z. — Abbreviation for Albin Wahl of Zella-Mehlis, Germany.

axq — WW-II German ordnance code assigned to Erfurter Laden Industrie, North Erfurt, Germany.

axs — WW-II German ordnance code assigned to Berndorfer Metallwarenfabrik AG, Berndorf, Austria (A. Krupp).

ay — WW-II German ordnance code assigned to Alois Pirkel, Electrotechnische Fabrik.

A Y A — Tradename of Aguirre y Aranzabal; Eibar, Spain from 1927. Makers of fine shotguns, now imported by Ventura.

ayf — WW-II German ordnance code assigned to Waffenfabrik Erma, Erfurt, Germany.

az — WW-II German ordnance code assigned to VDM-Halbzeugwerke, Altena, Germany.

AZANZA Y ARIZABALAGA — Pistol makers in Eibar, Spain, ca. 1916.

azg — WW-II German ordnance code assigned to Siemens-Schukert-Werke AG, Berlin, Germany.

AZUL — Tradename of Eulogio Arostegui.

azy — WW-II German ordnance code assigned to Mascinenfabrik Sangershausen.

B

"B" — Tradename used by Rohm on revolvers.

ba — WW-II German ordnance code assigned to Sundwiger Messingwerke, Iserlohn, Westphalia, Germany.

BABY — Model designation on .25 acp pistols used by F.N. on Brownings.

BABY HAMMERLESS — Model name used by Henry M. Kolb and his successor R.F. Sedgley on small revolvers.

BABY RUSSIAN — Tradename on revolvers used by the American Arms Co., ca. 1890.

BACKUP — Model designation used on pistols from T.D.E.

BACON ARMS CO. — Norwich, Conn. 1858-91. Made C.W. Hopkins revolvers, and Briggs & Hopkins revolvers, as well as many trade-named revolvers.

BAKER GUN CO. — Batavia, New York from 1903 until purchased by Crescent in 1933. Made shotguns, including the Batavia Leader.

BALLARD — Type of single-shot rifle made by Ball & Williams, 1861-66; Merrimack Arms & Mfg. Co., 1866-69; Brown Mfg. Co., 1869-73; and J. M. Marlin starting in 1875.

BALLARD & FAIRBANKS — Worcester, Mass. 1870-72, derringer makers and successor to C.H. Ballard & Co.

BALLISTER-MOLINA — Tradename of Hispano Argentine Fabrica de Automoviles Soc. Anonima.

BALLISTER-RIGAUD — Tradename of Hispano Argentine Fabrica de Automoviles Soc. Anonima.

BALTIMORE ARMS CO. — Baltimore, Md., maker of hammerless shotguns 1895-1902.

BANG-UP — Tradename used by Hopkins & Allen on revolvers, ca. 1880.

BARKER, T. — Tradename of shotguns made by Crescent Fire Arms Co., and also shotguns made in Belgium and imported by H & D Folsom Co.

BAR-STO PRECISION — Current manufacturer of stainless steel barrels and parts, manufacturer of pistols, ca. 1973.

BATAVIA LEADER — Tradename used on shotguns by the Baker Gun Co.

BAUER FIREARMS CORP. — Current manufacturer of pocket automatic pistols in Fraser, Mich.

BAYARD — Tradename of Anc. Etablissements Pieper, S.A.

BAY STATE ARMS CO. — Shotgun maker in Uxbridge and Worcester, Mass. 1873-74.

baz — WW-II German ordnance code assigned to Steyr-Daimler-Puch AG, Steyr, Austria.

bb — WW-II German ordnance code assigned to A. Laue & Co., Berlin, Germany.

B & B — Abbreviation for Braun & Bloem of Dusseldorf, Germany.

bc — WW-II German ordnance code assigned to Kupfer u. Messingwerke, Becker & Co. Langenberg, Germany.

B.C. — Trademark of Victor Bernedo y Cia.

bcd — WW-II German ordnance code assigned to Wilhelm-Gustloff-Werke, Weimar, Germany.

bck — WW-II German ordnance code assigned to Bruninghaus, Versmold, Germany.

bcu — WW-II German ordnance code assigned to Gutehohhnungshutte, Oberhausen, Germany.

bd — WW-II German ordnance code assigned to Metallwerke Lange AG, Bodenbach plant, Sudeten, Germany.

bda — WW-II German ordnance code assigned to Uhrenfabrik Villingen, Germany.

bdq — WW-II German ordnance code assigned to Ehrhardt & Kirsten, Koffer u. Lederwarenfabrik, Leipzig, Germany.

bdr — WW-II German ordnance code assigned to Richard Erhardt Lederwarenfabrik, Poeseneck, Germany.

bdy — WW-II German ordnance code assigned to Pittner, Leipzig, Germany.

be — WW-II German ordnance code assigned to Berndorfer Metallwarenfabrik, Berndorf, Austria (Krupp).

BECKER & HOLLANDER WAFFENBAU — Suhl, Germany from about 1915, made Beholla pistols. In 1920 Stenda Werke took over the production of the Boholla.

bed — WW-II German ordnance code assigned to Gustloffe-Werke, Weimar, Germany.

BEESLEY, FREDERICK — London, England; custom gunmaker from 1879 until merger with Joseph Lang & Co., Ltd. in 1900.

beh — WW-II German ordnance code assigned to Ernst Leitz, Wetzlar, Germany.

BEHOLLA — Tradename of Becker and Hollander.

bej — WW-II German ordnance code assigned to Maschinenfabrik Wolf, Buckau, Germany

bek — WW-II German ordnance code assigned to Hensoldt-Werk fur Optik u. Mechanik, Herborn, Germany.

BEKE — Tradename on rifles from Ferunion.

BELLMORE GUN CO. — Tradename used by Crescent Fire Arms Co. on shotguns.

BELMONT FIREARMS WORKS — See C.G. Bonehill, England.

BENELLI ARMI SpA — Current arms maker in Urbino, Italy. Imported by Diana Import Co.

BENEMERITA — Tradename used by D.F. Ortega de Seija of Madrid, Spain on pistols, ca. 1920.

BENET ARMS CO. — Importers of sporting arms in San Francisco, Calif. in the 1960's.

BERETTA, PIETRO — Current manufacturer of sporting arms with a company history that goes back to 1680 in Brescia, Italy.

BERGMANN, THEODOR — Manufacturer of pistols and machine guns from 1892 thru the end of WW-II, with many guns subcontracted to other makers. After Bergmann's death the firm was Gergmann Erben. Tradenames included Lignose.

BERKSHIRE — Tradename used by Shapleigh Hardware Co. of St. Louis, Mo.

BERLIN-SUHLER WAFFEN U. FAHRZENGWERKE — Pre-WW-II manufacturer of sporting and military arms in Berlin, Suhl, and Weimar, Germany.

BERNARDELLI, VINCENZO — Manufacturer of sporting arms in Brescia, Italy since 1865.

BESA — Tradename used by B.S.A.

BESCHI, MARIO — Manufacturer of shotguns in Italy, imported by J-K Imports, ca. 1970.

BESTIGUI HERMANOS — Manufacturers and distributors of revolvers and pistols in Eibar, Spain.

bf — WW-II German ordnance code assigned to Deutsche Rohenwerke AG, Muhlheim, Germany.

bfn — WW-II German ordnance code assigned to New York-Hamburger Gummifabrik.

bg — WW-II German ordnance code assigned to Enzesfelder Metallwerke, Vienna, Austria.

bh — WW-II German ordnance code assigned to Brunner Waffenfabrik, Brno, Czechoslovakia.

B.H. — Tradename of Beistegui Hermanos.

BICYCLE — Tradename on revolvers used by Harrington & Richardson.

BIG BONANZA — Tradename on spur trigger revolvers made by Bacon Arms Co., ca. 1880.

BIG HORN ARMS CO. — Watertown, S.D. Maker of unique single-shot pistols and shotguns that fired from an open bolt; exact dates of operation unknown.

BIJOU — Tradename of August Menz on pistols.

BIJOU — Tradename of D.D. Debouxtay on revolvers.

BIRMINGHAM SMALL ARMS CO. — see B.S.A.

BISON — Tradename on revolvers imported from Germany by Jana International, ca. 1971.

BITTNER, GUSTAV — Vejprty, Bohemiz, Austria-Hungary from 1893 until 1939. Manufactured a wide variety of firearms, but best known for his early repeating pistols.

BIVENS, JOHN — Custom replica rifle maker in Winston-Salem, N.C. since about 1970.

bj — WW-II German ordnance code assigned to Niebecker & Schumacher, Iserlohn, Germany.

bjm — WW-II German ordnance code assigned to Klockner Werke, Deutz plant, Germany.

bjv — WW-II German ordnance code assigned to Bohmisch-Mahrische Kolben-Danek AG, Vysocan plant, Prague, Czechoslovakia.

bk — WW-II German ordnance code assigned to Metall, Walz u. Plattierwarenfabrik Hinrichs & Auffermann AG, Wuppertal, Germany.

BKIW — Abbreviation for Berlin-Karlsruher Industrie Werke (name used by Deutsche Waffen u. Munitionsfabrik 1922-36).

bkp — WW-II German ordnance code assigned to Gewehrfabrik Burgsmuller & Sohn, Kreiensen, Germany.

bkq — WW-II German ordnance code assigned to Johannes Suremann GmbH Rohrenfabrik, Arnsbuerg, Germany.

bky — WW-II German ordnance code assigned to Bohmische Waffenfabrik AG, Prague, Ung.-Bro plant, Moravia, Czechoslovakia.

BLACK BEAUTY — Tradename used on shotguns made by Crescent Fire Arms Co. for Shapleigh Hdw. of St. Louis, Mo.

BLACKFIELD — Tradename used by Hibbard, Spencer, Bartlett Co. of Chicago, Ill.

blc — WW-II German ordnance code assigned to Carl Zeiss, Military Division, Jena, Germany.

BLISS & GOODYEAR — New Haven, Conn. from 1866 to 1887; makers of revolvers under a wide variety of brand names.

BLOODHOUND — Tradename used on revolvers by Hopkins & Allen, ca. 1880.

blp — WW-II German ordnance code assigned to Burgsmuller & Sohn, Kreiensen, Germany.

blu — WW-II German ordnance code assigned to Sprengstoffwerke, Blumenau near Felixdorf, Germany.

BLUE JACKET — Tradename used on revolvers by Hopkins & Allen, ca. 1880.

BLUE WHISTLER — Tradename used on revolvers by Hopkins & Allen, ca. 1880.

bmb — WW-II German ordnance code assigned to Metallwarenfabrik Binder, Reichertshofen, Germany.

bmd — WW-II German ordnance code assigned to Max G. Muller, Fabrik fur Lederwaren & Heeresbedarf, Nurnberg, Germany.

bmf — WW-II German ordnance code assigned to Berndorfer Metallwarenfabrik, Berndorf, Austria.

bmj — WW-II German ordnance code assigned to Hensoldt & Sohn, Mechanisch-Optische Werke AG, Wetzlar, Germany.

bmu — WW-II German ordnance code assigned to Carl Kuntze, Sattlerwarenfabrik, Penig, Germany.

bmv — WW-II German ordnance code assigned to Rheinmetall-Borsig AG, Sommerda plant, Germany.

bmz — WW-II German ordnance code assigned to Minerva-Nahmaschinenfabrik AG, Boskowitz, Czechoslovakia.

bnd — WW-II German ordnance code assigned to Maschinenfabrik Augsburg-Nurnberg, Nurnberg plant, Germany.

bne — WW-II German ordnance code assigned to Metallwarenfabrik Odertal GmbH, Odertal, Germany.

bnf — WW-II German ordnance code assigned to Polte, contract plant, Wolfenbuttel, Germany.

bnz — WW-II German ordnance code assigned to Steyr-Daimler-Puch AG, Steyr, Austria.

boa — WW-II German ordnance code assigned to Venditor, Troisdorf, Germany.

BOCH-DRILLING — Tradename used

by S. Gunther of Suhl, Germany in pre-WW-II Germany.

bod — WW-II German ordnance code assigned to Venditor, Troisdorf, Germany.

BOHMISCHE WAFFENFABRIK — German name for Ceska Zbrojovka (CZ).

BOLOMAUSER — Tradename used by Hy Hunter on pistols, ca. 1960.

BOLTON — Tradename of Francisco Arizmendi.

BOLUMBURU, GREGORIO — Pistol maker in Eibar, Spain, ca. 1920.

BONANCA — Tradename used by Bacon Arms Co. on revolvers.

BONEHILL, C.G. — Also known as Belmont Firearms Works in Birmingham, England since 1851.

BONEHILL, C.G. — Tradename used by H & D Folsom on shotguns made by Crescent Fire Arms Co. (U.S.).

BOSTON BULLDOG — Tradename used by J.P. Lovell & Sons on revolvers made by Iver Johnson.

bot — WW-II German ordnance code assigned to Metallwerke Neheim.

BOY'S CHOICE — Tradename used on revolvers from Hood Firearms Co., ca. 1875.

bpd — WW-II German ordnance code assigned to Optische Anstalt O.P. Gorz, Vienna, Austria.

bpr — WW-II German ordnance code assigned to Johannes Grossfuss, Metall u. Locierwarenfabrik, Dobeln, Germany.

bqo — WW-II German ordnance code assigned to Krupp-Gruson, Magdeburg-Buckau, Germany.

bqs — WW-II German ordnance code assigned to Oderhutte Kurstin.

bqt — WW-II German ordnance code assigned to Eugen Muller, Pyrotechnische Fabrik, Vienna, Austria.

br — WW-II German ordnance code assigned to Mathias Bauerle, Laufwerke GmbH, St. Georgen, Germany.

brd — WW-II German ordnance code assigned to Hagenuk, Neufelt & Kuhnke, Kiel, Germany.

BREDA, ERNESTO — Current manufacturer of sporting arms in Milan, Italy.

BRENNEKE GEWEHR U. GESCHOSSFABRIK — Manufacturer of firearms and bullets established in 1895 in Leipzig, Germany.

BRESCIA — Tradename on shotguns imported from Italy by Kleinguenther's of Seguin, Texas.

BRETTON — Current manufacturer of sporting arms in St. Etienne, France.

BREVEXSURESNES — Tradename on Brevex actions on rifles made in France and imported by Tradewinds.

B.R.F. — Initials unknown, successor to Pretoria Arms Factory.

BRIDGE GUN CO. — Tradename used by Shapleigh Hdw. of St. Louis, Mo. on shotguns made by Crescent Fire Arms Co.

BRIDGEPORT ARMS CO. — Tradename used by Fred Bifflar & Co. of Chicago, Ill.

BRISTOL — Tradename of Gregorio Bolumburu.

BRITISH BULLDOG — Tradename used by J.P. Lovell on revolvers made by Johnson, Bye & Co., ca. 1882.

BRNO — Tradename of Ceska Zbrojovka, Brno Works; from about 1922 to date.

BRONCHO — Tradename of A. Errasti.

BRONCO — Tradename of Echave y Arizmendi.

BRONCO — Tradename of Firearms International on single shot rifles and shotguns, ca. 1970.

BROWN PRECISION CO. — San Jose, Calif. Current manufacturer of fiberglass gunstocks and assembler of sporting and target rifles.

BROWNIE — Model designation used on pistols by O.F. Mossberg & Sons, ca. 1930.

BROWNING ARMS CO. — Current manufacturer and importer of arms under the Browning label in Morgan, Utah. Also see F.N.

BROWREDUIT — Tradename on revolvers from Salvador Arostegui.

BRUNSWIG — Tradename of Esperanza y Unceta (Astra).

BRUTUS — Tradename on revolvers from Hood Firearms Co., ca. 1875.

B.S.A. — Abbreviation and tradename for Birmingham Small Arms Co., Birmingham, England from 1885. Manufacturers of sporting rifles, shotguns, military rifles, and machineguns.

bsv — WW-II German ordnance code assigned to Tonshoff, Horn in Lippe, Germany.

BSW — Abbreviation for Belin-Suhler Waffen u. Fahrzengwerke.

BSW SELBSTLADE — Tradename of Berlin-Suhler Waffen und Fahrzeugwerke.

btk — WW-II German ordnance code assigned to Aluminium-Werke Honsel, Werdohl, Germany.

BUA — Abbreviation and tradename of Bolte u. Anschutz of Zella-Mehlis, Germany on pistols and rifles, ca. 1935.

buc — WW-II German ordnance code assigned to Metallwerke Windelsbleiche, near Bielefeld, Germany.

BUCK, A.H. & CO. — Manufacturer of single shot rifles in West Stafford, Conn. 1881-83.

BUDISCHOWSKI — Tradename of Norton Armament Corp. 1972-76.

BUFALO — Tradename of Gabilondo y Cia. on pistols.

BUFFALO — Tradename used on .22 western style revolvers made by Herbert Schmidt of West Germany.

BUFFALO BILL — Tradename on revolvers sold by Homer Fisher Co., ca. 1880.

BUFFALO-MATCH — Tradename on rifles made by Manufrance.

BUFFALO STAND — Tradename used on single-shot bolt action pistols made by Mre. Francaise d'Armes et Cycles.

buh — WW-II German ordnance code assigned to Rochling, Wetzler, Germany.

BUHAG — Tradename used by gunsmiths in Suhl, East Germany on target pistols.

BULLARD REPEATING ARMS CO. — Produced lever-action rifles in Springfield, Mass. from 1887 to 1889.

BULLDOG — Tradename on revolvers made by Forehand & Wadsworth, ca. 1880.

BULLDOG — Tradename on single shot "Hammond" pistols made by Conn. Arms & Mfg. Co.

BULL DOZER — Tradename used on single-shot Hammond Bulldog from Conn. Arms & Mfg. Co., ca. 1865.

BULL DOZER — Tradename on revolvers sold by J. McBride & Co., made by Norwich Falls Pistol Co., ca. 1975.

BULWARK — Tradename of Bestegui Hermanos.

BURGESS — Tradename used by Whitney Arms Co. on rifles, ca. 1880.

BURGESS GUN CO. — Shotgun maker in Buffalo, N.Y. 1893-95.

BURGHAM — Tradename of Mre. d'Armes des Pyrenees.

BURGO — Tradename used by K. Burgsmuller Sen. on Rohm revolvers.

BURY-DONCKIER — Tradename of custom sporting arms made in Belgium and imported by Continental Arms, ca. 1950.

BUSHMASTER — Model designation on guns made by Gwinn Arms Co. of Winston-Salem, N.C.

bvl — WW-II German ordnance code assigned to Theodor Bergmann & Co., Abteilung Automaten & Metallwarenfabrikation, Hamburg-Altona, Germany.

bwc — WW-II German ordnance code assigned to Maschinenfabrik Brackwede.

bwn — WW-II German ordnance code assigned to Krupp-Stahlwerk u. Maschinenfabrik, Essen, Germany.

bwo — WW-II German ordnance code assigned to Rheinmetall-Borsig AG, Dusseldorf, Germany.

bwp — WW-II German ordnance code assigned to Berlin-Anhaltische-Maschinenbau AG, Dessau, Germany.

bwr — WW-II German ordnance code assigned to Werk Lauchhammer.

bwx — WW-II German ordnance code assigned to Ruhrstahl, Heinrichshutte, Hattingen, Germany.

bxb — WW-II German ordnance code assigned to Skoda-Werke, Pilsen, Czechoslovakia.

bxe — WW-II German ordnance code assigned to Bochumer Verein.

bxm — WW-II German ordnance code assigned to Vereingte Zunder u. Kabelwerke, Meissen, Germany.

byc — WW-II German ordnance code assigned to Bruckenbauanstalt August Klonne AG, Dortmund, Germany.

bye — WW-II German ordnance code assigned to Hanomag, Hannover, Germany.

byf — WW-II German ordnance code assigned to Mauser-Werke, Oberndorf am Neckar, Germany.

byg — WW-II German ordnance code assigned to Johann Wyksen, Optische u. Feinmaschinen, Katowitz, Poland.

bym — WW-II German ordnance code assigned to Genossenschafts-Maschinenhaus der Buchsenmacher, Ferlach, Austria.

byq — WW-II German ordnance code assigned to Pohlmann & Co., Hammerwerke, Wetterburg, Hessen-Nassau, Germany.

byr — WW-II German ordnance code assigned to Ruhrstahl, Witten-Annen, Germany.

bys — WW-II German ordnance code assigned to Ruhrstahl, Witten, Germany.

byw — WW-II German ordnance code assigned to Johann Schafer, Stettiner Schraubenwerk, Stetten, Germany.

bzt — WW-II German ordnance code assigned to Fritz Wolf, Gewehrfabrik, Zella-Mehlis, Germany.

C

ca — WW-II German ordnance code assigned to Vereinigte Deutsche Nickelwerke, Schwerte, Ruhr, Germany.

CADET — Tradename on revolvers sold by Maltby-Curtis & Co., ca. 1885.

cag — WW-II German ordnance code assigned to Swarowski Glasfabrik u. Tyrolit, Wattens, Tyrol, Austria.

C.A.L. — Abbreviation for Carbine Automatique Legere, a carbine made by F.N.

CAMPEON — Tradename of Hijos de C. Arrizabalaga on handguns.

CAMPO GIRO — Spanish military pistol made by Esperanza y Unceta (Astra).

CANTABRIA — Tradename of Garate Hermanos on handguns.

CAP-CHUR — Tradename used by Palmer Chemical & Equipment Co. of Douglasville, Ga., manufacturer of animal control and tranquilizing equipment.

CAPITAN — Tradename of Mre. d'Armes des Pyrenees on pistols.

CAPT. JACK — Tradename used by Hopkins & Allen on revolvers, ca. 1880.

CAROLINA ARMS CO. — Tradename on shotguns made by Crescent Firearms Co. for Smith-Wadsworth Hardware Co. of Charlotte, N.C.

CATTLEMAN — Tradename on single action revolvers made by A. Uberti of Italy.

CBC — Abbreviation and tradename used by Compania Brazileira de Cartuchos on shotguns imported by F.I.E.

cbl — WW-II German ordnance code assigned to VDM-Halberwerkzeuge, Nurnberg branch, Germany.

cbr — WW-II German ordnance code assigned to Bohlerwerk, Bohler & Co., Waidhofen, Austria.

cby — WW-II German ordnance code assigned to Scholler-Blechmann,

Ternitz, Niederdonau, Germany.

ccb — WW-II German ordnance code assigned to Stahlwerke Brunninghaus AG, Westhofen, Germany.

ccd — WW-II German ordnance code assigned to DEMAG, Wetter, Germany.

ccx — WW-II German ordnance code assigned to Optische u. Feinmaschinewerke, Hugo Meyer & Co., Gorlitz, Germany.

cdc — WW-II German ordnance code assigned to Kern, Klager & Co. Lederwaren, Berlin, Germany.

cdg — WW-II German ordnance code assigned to Auwarter & Bubeck Lederwarenfabrik, Stuttgart, Germany.

cdo — WW-II German ordnance code assigned to Theodor Bergmann & Co., Waffen u. Munitionsfabrik, Velten plant, Velten am Main, Germany.

cdp — WW-II German ordnance code assigned to Theodor Bergmann & Co., Waffen u. Munitionsfabrik, Bernau plant, Berlin, Germany.

cdv — WW-II German ordnance code assigned to Metallwarenfabrik Ludwig Maybaum, Sundern, Germany.

ce — WW-II German ordnance code assigned to J. P. Sauer & Sohn, Waffenfabrik, Suhl, Germany.

CEBRA — Tradename of Arizmendi, Zulaika y Cia. on pistols.

CEBRA — Tradename on revolvers from Antonio Errasti.

CELTA — Tradename used by Tomas de Urizar y Cia. of Eibar, Spain, ca. 1935.

CENTAUR — Tradename on shotguns imported from Belgium by Continental Arms.

CENTENNIAL — Tradename used by Deringer Rifle & Pistol Works on revolvers, ca. 1876.

CENTRAL — Tradename used by J. Stevens Arms Co. on shotguns.

CENTRAL ARMS CO. — Tradename on shotguns used by Shapleigh Hdw. Co. of St. Louis, Mo. on guns made by Crescent Firearms Co.

CENTURON — Tradename on rifles imported by Golden State Arms Co. and assembled by Pasedina Arms Corp., ca. 1960.

CENTURY ARMS CO. — Importers of military and sporting arms since the 1950's in St. Albans, Vt.

CESAR J. — Tradename of Tomas de Urizar y Cia.

CETME — Abbreviation for Centro de Estudios Tecnicos de Materiales Especiales of Madrid, Spain, and name of model of rifle that they developed.

cey — WW-II German ordnance code assigned to Karl Budischovsky & Sohne, Osterreichische Lederindustrie AG, Vienna, Austria.

cf — WW-II German ordnance code assigned to Westfalische Anhaltische Sprengstoff, Oranienburg plant, Germany.

cg — WW-II German ordnance code assigned to Finower Industrie GmbH, Finow, Mark, Germany.

C.G.H. — Abbreviation for C.G. Haenel.

cgn — WW-II German ordnance code assigned to Rohrbacher Lederfabrik, Josef Poschels Sohne, Rohrbach, Germany.

ch — WW-II German ordnance code assigned to Fabrique National d'Armes de Guerre, Herstal, Liege, Belgium.

C.H. — Abbreviation for Crucelegui Hermanos.

CHALLENGE — Tradename used on revolvers made by Bliss & Goodyear, ca. 1875.

CHAMPION — Model name used by Iver Johnson on shotguns.

CHAMPION — Tradename used by John Powell & Son of Cincinnati, Ohio, ca. 1890.

CHAMPLIN FIREARMS, INC. — Current importer and manufacturer of sporting arms in Enid, Okla.

CHANTICLER — Tradename of I. Charola on handguns (Spain).

CHANTICLER — Tradename of Mre. d'Armes des Pyrenees on pistols (France).

CHARTER ARMS CORP. — Current manufacturer of firearms in Stratford, Conn.

chd — WW-II German ordnance code assigned to Deutsche Industrie-Werke AG, Berlin-Spandau, Germany.

CHEROKEE ARMS CO. — Tradename used by C.M. McClung & Co. of Knoxville, Tenn. on shotguns made by Crescent Firearms Co.

CHESAPEAKE GUN CO. — Tradename on shotguns made by Crescent Firearms Co.

chh — WW-II German ordnance code assigned to DEW, Hannover plant, Linden, Germany.

CHICAGO ARMS CO. — Tradename used by Fred Bifflar Co. of Chicago, Ill. on revolvers made by Meridan Firearms Co.

CHICAGO FIRE ARMS CO. — Chicago, Ill. late 1880's to 1893. Manufactured "Protector" palm pistols.

CHICNESTER — Tradename used on revolvers by Hopkins & Allen, ca. 1880.

CHIEFTAIN — Tradename on revolvers made by Norwich Falls Pistol Co., ca. 1880.

CHIMERE REINOR — Tradename of Mre. d'Armes des Pyrenees on pistols.

CHURCHILL, E. J. LTD. — Custom gunmakers in London, England. From 1869 to 1892 the company was called Charles Churchill, the name was changed to its current form in 1892. Also known as Churchill Gun Makers Ltd.

CHYLEWSKI — Tradename of "einhand" pistols made by Soc. Industrielle Suisse and Bergmann & Lignose.

cjn — WW-II German ordnance code assigned to Uhrenfabrik, Gebruder Junghans, Schramberg, Germany.

ck — WW-II German ordnance code assigned to Metallwerk Neumeyer, Munich, Germany.

ckc — WW-II German ordnance code assigned to Deutsche Eisenwerke AG, Muhlheim, Ruhr, Germany.

ckl — WW-II German ordnance code

assigned to Eisen u. Huttenwerke, Thale, Harz, Germany.

cko — WW-II German ordnance code assigned to Huttenwerk, Eisengiesserei u. Maschinenfabrik, Michelstadt, Odenwalt, Germany.

cl — WW-II German ordnance code assigned to Metschke Karl, Auto u. Maschinenreparatur, Berlin plant, Germany.

CLASSIC ARMS — Importers and manufacturers of blackpowder guns and kits, located in Palmer, Mass. Purchased by Val Forgett of Navy Arms in 1978.

CLEMENT, CHARLES — Pistol and revolver manufacturer in Liege, Belgium about 1886 to 1914.

CLERKE — Current manufacturers of revolvers in Santa Monica, Calif.

CLIMAS — Tradename used by J. Stevens Arms Co. on shotguns.

CLIMAX — Tradename used on handguns by J. Palmer, O'Neal & Co. of Pittsburgh, Pa.

CLUB — Tradename on rifles made by Manufrance.

cmg — WW-II German ordnance code assigned to Metallwarenfabrik Halver, Peter W. Haurand GmbH Halver, Westphalia, Germany.

cms — WW-II German ordnance code assigned to Konrad Lindhorst, Berlin, Germany.

cmw — WW-II German ordnance code assigned to Dr. Ing, Rudolf Hell, Berlin, Germany.

cmz — WW-II German ordnance code assigned to Zunderwerke Ernst Brun, Krefeld, Linn, Germany.

cna — WW-II German ordnance code assigned to Krupp-National-Registrierkassen, Berlin, Germany.

cnd — WW-II German ordnance code assigned to Krupp-National-Registrierkassen, GmbH, Berlin, Germany.

COAST TO COAST — Tradename used by U.S. chain of hardware stores of the same name on sporting arms.

cob — WW-II German ordnance code assigned to Netzschkauer Maschinenfabrik, Stark & Sohne, Netzschkau, Saxony, Germany.

COBOLT — Tradename of L. Ancion Marx on revolvers.

CODY MANUFACTURING CORP. — Revolver maker in Chicopee, Mass. after WW-II. Made "Thunderbird" revolvers.

coe — WW-II German ordnance code assigned to Lubecker Maschinenbau-Gesellschaft.

cof — WW-II German ordnance code assigned to Waffenfabrik Eikhorn, Solingen, Germany.

COGSWELL & HARRISON — Gunmakers in London, England from 1770 to date. From 1924 to 1938 had a branch in Paris, France.

COLLATH — Tradename used by Teschner-Collath of Frankfurt, Germany, ca. 1930.

COLON — Tradename of Antonio Azpiri.

COLONIAL — Tradename of Fab. d'Armes de Guerre de Grande Precision on pistols (Spain).

COLONIAL — Tradename of Mre. d'Armes des Pyrenees on pistols (Belgium).

COLTON FIREARMS CO. — Tradename used by Sears, Roebuck & Co.

COLUMBIAN — Tradename of revolvers made by Foehl & Weeks, ca. 1890.

COMMANDO ARMS — Current manufacturer of carbines in Knoxville, Tenn. Distributed by Volunteer Enterprises, Inc.

COMMERCIAL CONTROLS CORP. — Successor to National Postal Meter, manufacturer of M-1 Carbines, ca. WW-II in Rochester, N.Y.

COMPEER — Tradename used by Van Camp Hdw. of Indianapolis, Indiana on firearms made by Crescent Firearms Co.

COMPETITION — Tradename used by John Meunier Gun Co. of Milwaukee, Wisc.

con — WW-II German ordnance code assigned to Franz Stock, Maschinen u. Werkzeugfabrik, Berlin, Germany.

CONNECTICUT ARMS & MFG CO. — Naubuc and Glastenbury, Conn. 1863-68. Makers of the single shot Hammond pistol and carbine.

CONNECTICUT VALLEY ARMS CO. — Current manufacturer and importer of blackpowder arms and firearms kits in Haddon, Conn.

CONQUEROR — Tradename on revolvers made by Bacon Arms Co., ca. 1880.

CONSTABLER — Tradename of Mre. Liegeoise d'Armes a Feu on revolvers.

CONTINENTAL — Tradename used on rifles and shotguns by J. Stevens Arms Co.

CONTINENTAL — Tradename used by Hood Firearms Co. on revolvers sold by Marshall Wells & Co., ca. 1870.

CONTINENTAL — Tradename of M. Neumann on handguns (Belgium).

CONTINENTAL — Tradename of Reheinische Waffen und Munitionsfabrik on pistols (Germany).

CONTINENTAL — Tradename of Tomas de Urizar y Cia. on pistols (Spain).

CONTINENTAL ARMS — Importers of sporting arms in N.Y.C. from the mid-1950's until 1965.

COPELAND, FRANK — Revolver maker in Worcester, Mass. 1868-74.

CORLA — Tradename of Fab. de Armas Zaragoza.

CORRIENTES — Tradename of Modesto Santos.

cos — WW-II German ordnance code assigned to Gebruder Merz, Merz-Werke, Frankfurt, Germany.

COSMOPOLITE OSCILLATORY — Tradename used on copies of S & W revolvers by Garate, Anitua y Cia.

COUNET — Tradename on revolvers from Auguste Francotte et Cie.

cow — WW-II German ordnance code assigned to Wintershall AG, Spritzgusswerk, Berlin, Germany.

COW BOY — Tradename of Fabrication Francaise on pistols.

COW BOY RANGER — Tradename used on revolvers by Liege United Arms Co.

cpn — WW-II German ordnance code assigned to Werk Apolda.

cpo — WW-II German ordnance code assigned to Rheinmetall-Borsig AG, Berlin-Marienfeld, Germany.

cpp — WW-II German ordnance code assigned to Rheinmetall-Borsig AG, Breslau plant.

cpq — WW-II German ordnance code assigned to Rheinmetall -Borsig AG, Bubeb plant.

cq — WW-II German ordnance code assigned to Warz & Co., Zella-Mehlis, Germany.

CREEDMORE — Tradename used on revolvers by Hopkins & Allen, ca. 1880.

CRESCENT — Tradename used on revolvers by Norwich Falls Pistol Co., ca. 1880.

CRIOLLA — Tradename of Hispano Argentine Fab. de Automoviles on pistols.

CRISTOBAL — Tradename on arms made by Armeria Fabrica de Armas, San Cristobal, Dominican Republic.

crm — WW-II German ordnance code assigned to PhyWE, Gottingen, Germany.

cro — WW-II German ordnance code assigned to R. Fuess Optische Industrie, Berlin-Steglitz, Germany.

CROWN CITY ARMS — Distributors for Essex Arms Corp. and pistol makers; in current operation in Cortland, N.Y.

CROWN JEWEL — Tradename used on revolvers by Norwich Falls Pistol Co., ca. 1880.

crs — WW-II German ordnance code assigned to Fritz Werner, Plant II, Berlin, Germany.

CRUCELEGUI — Tradename of Hijos de C. Arrizabalaga on pistols made for Crucelegui Hermanos.

CRUSO — Tradename on rifles and shotguns used by J. Stevens Arms Co.

CRUSO — Tradename used by Hibbard, Spencer, Bartlett Co. on shotguns made by Crescent Fire Arms Co.

crw — WW-II German ordnance code assigned to Maschinenfabrik Hofmann GmbH, Breslau.

csa — WW-II German ordnance code assigned to Skoda-Werke.

csq — WW-II German ordnance code assigned to Pollux, Ludwigshafen, Rhein, Germany.

csx — WW-II German ordnance code assigned to Gothaer Metallwarenfabrik GmbH.

cte — WW-II German ordnance code assigned to Klockner Maschinenfabrik, Manstadt division, Troisdorf, Germany.

ctf — WW-II German ordnance code assigned to Eisenwerke Gaggenau GmbH, Gaggenau, Germany.

ctg — WW-II German ordnance code assigned to Karlshutte Waldenburg, Altwasser, Germany.

ctn — WW-II German ordnance code assigned to Freidricks & Co., Hanseatische Werkstatten fur Feinmeckanik u. Optik.

cts — WW-II German ordnance code assigned to Markische Werke, H. Hillmann GmbH, Halver, Germany.

cue — WW-II German ordnance code assigned to Rochlinf-Buderus-Stahlwerke, Finofurt plant, Brandenburg, Germany.

cuf — WW-II German ordnance code assigned to Rochling-Buderus-Stahlwerke, Melle plant, Hannover, Germany.

CUMBERLAND ARMS CO. — Tradename used by Grey & Dudley Hardware Co. of Nashville, Tenn. on shotguns made by Crescent Fire Arms Co.

cuz — WW-II German ordnance code assigned to Eisenwerk Maximilianhutte, Unterwellenborn. Thuringia, Germany.

cva — WW-II German ordnance code assigned to Eisenwerke Maximilianhutte, Fronberg, Germany.

C.V.A. — Abbreviation for Connecticut Valley Arms Co.

cvb — WW-II German ordnance code assigned to Otto Sindel, Lederwarenfabrik, Berlin, Germany.

cvc — WW-II German ordnance code assigned to Zeschke Nachfolge Gebruder L. Zeuschner, Koffer u Lederwarenfabrik, Mullrose near Frankfurt am Oder, Germany.

cvg — WW-II German ordnance code assigned to VDM, Frankfurt-Hedderheim, Germany.

cvl — WW-II German ordnance code assigned to WKC Waffenfabrik, Solingen Wald, Germany.

cvs — WW-II German ordnance code assigned to Paul Weyersberg & Co., Waffenfabrik, Solingen, Germany.

cvv — WW-II German ordnance code assigned to Maschinenfabrik B. Holthaus, Dinklage, Germany.

cwb — WW-II German ordnance code assigned to Brandenburger Eisenwerke, Brandenburg, Germany.

cwg — WW-II German ordnance code assigned to Westfalisch-Anhaltisce Sprengstoff AG, Coswig plant, Germany.

cww — WW-II German ordnance code assigned to Karl Weiss, Lederwarenfabrik, Braunschweig, Germany.

cxa — WW-II German ordnance code assigned to Ruhrstahl AG, Stahlwerk Krieger, Dusseldorf-Oberhausen, Germany.

cxd — WW-II German ordnance code assigned to Maschinenfabrik Becker & Co., Magdeburg, Germany.

cxg — WW-II German ordnance code assigned to Metallwarenfabrik Spreewerk AG, Berlin-Spandau, Germany.

cxh — WW-II German ordnance code assigned to Kienzle, Schwenningen am Neckar, Germany.

cxm — WW-II German ordnance code assigned to Gustav Genschow & Co., Berlin, Germany.

cxn — WW-II German ordnance code assigned to Emil Busch AG, Optische Industrie, Rathenow, Germany.

cxq — WW-II German ordnance code

assigned to Spreewerke GmbH, Metallwarenfabrik, Berlin-Spandau, Germany.

cyd - WW-II German ordnance code assigned to Nottebohm, Ludenscheid, Germany.

cyh — WW-II German ordnance code assigned to Huttenwerke Siegerland, Eichner, Germany.

cyq — WW-II German ordnance code assigned to Spreewerke GmbH, Metallwarenfabrik, Berlin-Spandau, Germany.

CZ — Tradename of Ceska Zbrojovka.

CZAR — Tradename used on revolvers by Hopkins & Allen, ca. 1880.

CZAR — Tradename on revolvers made by Hood Firearms, ca. 1875.

czf — WW-II German ordnance code assigned to Maschinenfabrik Steubing & Co., Berlin, Germany.

czm — WW-II German ordnance code assigned to Gustav Genschow & Co., Berlin, Germany.

czn — WW-II German ordnance code assigned to Emil Busch AG, Optische Industrie, Rathenow, Germany.

czo — WW-II German ordnance code assigned to Heereszeugamt, Geschosswerkstatt, Konigsberg, Germany.

czq — WW-II German ordnance code assigned to Schichau-Elbing, Konigsberg division, Germany.

czs — WW-II German ordnance code assigned to Brennabor Werke AG, Brandenburg, Germany.

D

dah — WW-II German ordnance code assigned to Junkers, Dessau, Germany.

DAINO — Tradename on single shot shotguns imported by Kleinfuenther's of Seguin, Texas.

DAISY — Tradename on revolvers from Bacon Arms Co., ca. 1880.

DAKIN GUN CO. — Importers of Italian and Spanish Shotguns, ca. 1960 in San Francisco, Calif.

DAKOTA — Tradename on revolvers made by Uberti.

DALY ARMS CO. — Revolver maker in New York City, ca. 1890.

DANIEL BOONE GUN CO. — Tradename used by Belknap Hardware of Louisville, Ky. on shotguns.

DANTON — Tradename of Gabilondo y Cia.

DAN WESSON ARMS CO. — Current manufacturer of revolvers with a unique barrel takedown system in Monson, Mass.

dar — WW-II German ordnance code assigned to Metallindustrie Schonbeck AG, Schonbeck am Elbe, Germany.

DARDICK CORP. — Manufacturers of unusual revolving carrier pistols in Hamden, Conn.

DAREDEVIL — Tradename used by Lou J. Eppinger, Inc. of Detroit, Mich.

DARNE — Manufacturer of sporting arms since 1881 in St. Etienne, France.

DAUDETAU, L. — Name of a series of French military rifles, ca. 1900 and named for their inventor.

DAVENPORT, W.H. ARMS CO. — Manufacturer of rifles and shotguns in Norwich, Conn. 1855-1910.

DAVIDSON FIREARMS CO. — Importers of shotguns made by Fabrica de Armas in Spain; located in Greensboro, N.C.

DAVIS, N.R. & CO. — Freetown, Mass. 1853-1917. In 1917 merged with Warner Arms Co. and changed the name to Davis-Warner Arms Co., and became inactive about 1921. In 1930 merged with Crescent Fire Arms Co. and became Crescent-Davis Arms Co. Was purchased by J. Stevens Arms Co. in 1932.

DAVIS-WARNER ARMS CO. — Name of merged N.R. Davis & Co. and Warner Arms Corp., Norwich, Conn. 1917-30, though inactive from about 1921 until it was merged with Crescent Fire Arms Co. to form Crescent-Davis Arms Corp. in 1930.

DAY ARMS CO. — Distributors for Essex Arms Corp. and makers of pistols and M1911 modifications; in current operation in San Antonio, Tex.

daz — WW-II German ordnance code assigned to Maximilianhutte, plant II, Unterwellenborn, Thuringia, Germany.

dbg — WW-II German ordnance code assigned to Dynamit AG (Alfred Nobel & Co.), Duneberg plant.

dbh — WW-II German ordnance code assigned to Mannesmann, Dusseldorf plant, Germany.

dde — WW-II German ordnance code assigned to Robert Larsen, Fabrik fur Leder u. Stoffwaren, Berlin, Germany.

ddx — WW-II German ordnance code assigned to Voigtlander u. Sohn AG, Braunschweig, Germany.

dea — WW-II German ordnance code assigned to Frankfurter Maschinenbau, Pokorny & Wittekind, Frankfurt, Germany.

DEAD SHOT — Tradename on revolvers used by L.W. Pond Co.

dec — WW-II German ordnance code assigned to Bleiwerk Goslar.

DEFENDER — Tradename on revolvers made for J.P. Lovell Arms by Iver Johnson, ca. 1880.

DEFENDER — Trademark on pistols used by Javier Echaniz.

DEFIANCE — Tradename on revolvers made by Norwich Falls Pistol Co., ca. 1880.

DEK-DU — Tradename of Tomas de Urizar y Cia.

DELPHIAN — Tradename used by J. Stevens Arms Co. on shotguns.

DELPHIAN — Tradename used by Supplee-Biddle Hardware Co. of Philadelphia, Pa.

DELU — Tradename of Fab. d'Armes Delu & Co.

DeLUXE — Tradename of Gregorio Bolumburu.

DEMON MARINE — Tradename of Mre. d'Armes des Pyrenees.

DERINGER RIFLE AND PISTOL WORKS — Philadelphia, Pa. 1873-79.

Successor to Henry Deringer, Jr. and formed after his death.

DESPATCH — Tradename used by Hopkins & Allen on revolvers, ca. 1875.

DESTROYER — Tradename of Isidro Gaztanaga on pistols.

DESTROYER CARBINES — Spanish police carbines made by Gaztanaga y Cia, of Eibar, Spain, ca. 1925, and more recently Ayra Duria S.A. of Eibar, Spain.

DESTRUCTOR — Tradename of Retolaza Hermanos on pistols.

DETECTIVE — Tradename of Garate, Anitua y Cia. on revolvers (Spain).

DETECTIVE REVOLVER — Tradename used by Hy Hunter of Burbank, Calif. on imported revolvers, ca. 1960.

DETONICS, INC. — Current manufacturer of pistols in Seattle, Wash.

DEUTSCHE SELBSTLADE PISTOLE — Tradename on pistols from Gotthilf von Nordheim of Zella-Mehlis, Germany, 1929-39.

DEUTSCHE WAFFENFABRIK GEORG KNAAK — See Georg Knaak.

dev — WW-II German ordnance code assigned to DEW, Remscheid plant, Germany.

dfb — WW-II German ordnance code assigned to Gustloff Co., Waffenfabrik, Suhl, Germany.

DGA — Tradename of Shilen Rifles, Inc. on rifle actions.

dgb — WW-II German ordnance code assigned to Dynamit AG, (Alfred Nobel & Co.), Duneberg plant.

dgl — WW-II ordnance code assigned to Remo Gewehrfabrik, Gebruder Rempt, Suhl, Germany.

dgz — WW-II German ordnance code assigned to Bohler, Kapfenberg, Austria.

dha — WW-II German ordnance code assigned to Krupp, Hannover plant, Germany.

dhp — WW-II German ordnance code assigned to H. Burgsmuller, Gewehrfabrik, Kreiensen-Harz, Germany.

DIAMOND — Tradename used by J. Stevens Arms Co. on shotguns.

DIAMOND ARMS CO. — Tradename used by Shapleigh Hardware Co. of St. Louis, Mo.

DIANE — Tradename on pistols made by Wilkinson Arms, ca. 1976.

DICKINSON, E. L. & CO. — Revolver makers in Springfield, Mass. 1870-80.

DICKSON BULLDOG — Tradename on revolvers used by Herman Weihrauch Sportwaffenfabrik.

DICKSON SPECIAL AGENT — Tradename used by Echave, Arizmendi y Cia. on pistols.

DICTATOR — Tradename on revolvers from Hopkins & Allen, ca. 1880.

DICTATOR — Tradename on pistols of Soc. Anonyme des Fab. d'Armes Reunies.

DIXIE GUN WORKS — Importer and manufacturer of blackpowder guns and kits in Union City, Tenn.

djf — WW-II German ordnance code assigned to Draht-Bremer, Rostock, Mecklenburg, Germany.

dkk — WW-II German ordnance code assigned to Friedrich Offerman & Sohne, Lederwarenfabrik, Bensberg, Germany.

dla — WW-II German ordnance code assigned to Karl Barth, Militareffekten-Fabrik, Waldbrohl, Germany.

dld — WW-II German ordnance code assigned to Kromag, Hirtenberg, Austria.

dlu — WW-II German ordnance code assigned to Ewald Lunenschloss, Militareffecten-Fabrik, Solingen, Germany.

dma — WW-II German ordnance code assigned to Heeresmunitionsanstalt u. Geschosswerkstatt, Zeithain, Germany.

dmk — WW-II German ordnance code assigned to Ilseder Hutte, Peiner, Germany.

dmo — WW-II German ordnance code assigned to Auto-Union, Chemnitz, Czechoslovakia.

dmy — WW-II German ordnance code assigned to Fritz Werner, Berlin-Marienfeld, Germany.

dn — WW-II German ordnance code assigned to Vereingte Deutsche Nickelwerke, Laband, Germany.

dnf — WW-II German ordnance code assigned to Rheinische-Westfalische Sprengstoff AG, Stadeln near Nurnberg, Germany.

dnh — WW-II German ordnance code assigned to Rheinische-Westfalische Sprengstoff AG, Durlach, Germany.

dnz — WW-II German ordnance code assigned to Schwarzwalder Apparatenbauanstalt, August Schwek & Sohne, Villingen, Germany.

dom — WW-II German ordnance code assigned to Westfalische Metallindustrie, Lippstadt, Germany.

dot — WW-II German ordnance code assigned to Waffenwerke Brunn, Brunn plant, Czechoslovakia.

dou — WW-II German ordnance code assigned to Waffenwerke Brunn, Bystrica, Czechoslovakia.

DOUGLAS — Tradename of Lasagabaster Hermanos on handguns.

dov — WW-II German ordnance code assigned to Waffenwerke Brunn, Vsetin, Czechoslovakia.

dow — WW-II German ordnance code assigned to Waffenwerke Brunn, Prerau, Czechoslovakia (Optotechnica AG).

dox — WW-II German ordnance code assigned to Waffenwerke Brunn, Podbrezova, Czechoslovakia.

dph — WW-II German ordnance code assigned to I.G. Farbenindustrie AG, Autogen plant, Frankfurt, Germany.

dpk — WW-II German ordnance code assigned to Hagenuk, Berlin-Tempelhof, Germany.

dpl — WW-II German ordnance code assigned to Remo Gewehrfabrik, Gebruder Rempt, Suhl, Germany.

dpm — WW-II German ordnance code assigned to Poldi-Hutte, Komotau, Sedeten, Germany.

dps — WW-II German ordnance code assigned to Auto-Union, Mittweida, Germany.

dpu — WW-II German ordnance code assigned to Schlothauer GmbH, Metallwaren, Ruhla, Germany.

dpw — WW-II German ordnance code assigned to Zeiss-Ikon, Gorz plant, Berlin-Zehlendorf, Germany.

dpx — WW-II German ordnance code assigned to Zeiss-Ikon, Stuttgart, Germany.

DREADNAUGHT — Trademark used on revolvers by Hopkins & Allen, ca. 1880.

DREADNAUGHT — Tradename on revolvers from Antonio Errasti (Spain).

DREYSE — Tradename of Rheinische Metallwaren und Maschinenfabrik on pistols.

D.R.G.M. — Abbreviation for Deutsches Reichs-Gerrauchs Muster (German registered design).

DRULOV — Tradename on Czech target pistols marketed by Omnipol.

drv — WW-II German ordnance code assigned to HASAG, Tschenstochau.

DSCHULLNIG — Tradename on rifles imported by Firearms Center of Spokane, Wash.; guns are made in Austria.

dsh — WW-II German ordnance code assigned to Ingenieur F. Janecek, Gewehrfabrik, Prague, Czechoslovakia.

dsj — WW-II German ordnance code assigned to WAMA Metallwerke, Oberlungwitz, Germany.

dsx — WW-II German ordnance code assigned to Rochling-Buderus, Wetzlar, Germany.

dta — WW-II German ordnance code assigned to A. Waldhausen, Inhaber M. Bruchmann, Sattler u. Kofferfabrik, Cologne, Germany.

dtu — WW-II German ordnance code assigned to G.J. Ensink & Co., Spezialfabrik fur Militarausrustung, Ohrdruf, Germany.

dtv — WW-II German ordnance code assigned to C. Otto Gehrkens, Leder u. Riemenwerke, Pinneberg, Germany.

DUAN — Tradename of Fernando Ormachea on handguns.

DU BIEL ARMS CO. — Current manufacturer of sporting rifles in Sherman, Texas.

DUCO — Tradename used by Fs. Dumoulin et Cie.

DUMOULIN FRERES ET CIE. — Manufacturers of firearms in Liege, Belgium from 1849.

dun — WW-II German ordnance code assigned to Poldi Hutte, Kladno, Czechoslovakia.

DUNLAP SPECIAL — Tradename used by Dunlap Hardware Co. of Macon, Ga. on arms made by Davis-Warner Arms Corp.

DUO — Tradename of Fr. Dusek on pistols (Czechoslovakia).

DUPLEX — Tradename used by Osgood Gun Works of Norwich, Conn. on revolvers, ca. 1882.

duv — WW-II German ordnance code assigned to Berliner-Lubecker Maschinenfabrik, Lubeck plant, Germany.

duw — WW-II German ordnance code assigned to Deutsche Rohrwerk AG, Mulheim, Germany.

dvr — WW-II German ordnance code assigned to Johann Prohlich, Lederwarenfabrik, Vienna, Austria.

dvu — WW-II German ordnance code assigned to Schichau, Elbing.

dwm — WW-II German ordnance code assigned to Deutsche Waffen u. Munitiounswerke, Berlin-Borsigwalde, Germany.

D.W.M. — Abbreviation for Deutsche Waffen und Munitionsfabriken.

dxs — WW-II German ordnance code assigned to Thyssen, Duisburg-Hamborn, Germany.

dye — WW-II German ordnance code assigned to Ed. Pitschmann, Pyrotechnik, Innsbruck, Austria.

dym — WW-II German ordnance code assigned to Runge & Kaulfuss, Rathenow, Germany.

dyq — WW-II German ordnance code assigned to DEW, Werdohl plant, Germany.

dza — WW-II German ordnance code assigned to Bleiwerke Dr. Schulcke, Hamburg, Germany.

dzl — WW-II German ordnance code assigned to Optische Anstalt Oigee, Berlin, Germany.

dzw — WW-II German ordnance code assigned to Metallwerke v. Galkowsky & Kielblock, Finow.

E

E.A. — Abbreviation for Echave y Arizmendi of Eibar, Spain.

eaf — WW-II German ordnance code assigned to Mechanoptik-Gesellschaft fur Prazisionstechnik, Aude & Reipe, Babelsberg, Germany.

EAGLE — Tradename used on revolvers by Iver Johnson, ca. 1880.

EAGLE GUN CO. — Carbine manufacturer in Stratford, Conn., ca. 1965.

eah — WW-II German ordnance code assigned to Bruninghaus, Werdohl, Germany.

eak — WW-II German ordnance code assigned to Deutsche Werke Kiel, Germany.

ean — WW-II German ordnance code assigned to Eisen- u. Metallwerke, Lippstadt, Germany.

EARLHOOD — Tradename on revolvers made by E.L. Dickinson Co., ca 1880.

EARTHQUAKE — Tradename on revolvers made by E.L. Dickinson, ca. 1880.

EASTERN — Tradename used by J. Stevens Arms Co. on shotguns.

EASTERN ARMS CO. — Tradename used by Sears, Roebuck & Co. on revolvers made by Meriden Firearms.

EASTFIELD — Tradename used by Smith & Wesson on shotguns.

eba — WW-II German ordnance code assigned to Scharfenberg & Teubert GmbH, Metallwarenfabrik, Breitungen.

ebf — WW-II German ordnance code assigned to Huttenwerke Siegerland, Charlottenhutte plant, Wiederschelden.

ecc — WW-II German ordnance code assigned to Oskar Lunig, Pyrotechnische Fabrik, Mohringen.

ecd — WW-II German ordnance code assigned to Graf Lippold, Pyrotechnische Fabrik, Wuppertal-Elberfeld.

ECHASA — Tradename of Echave, Arizmendi y Cia. on pistols.

ECKO — Tradename of Emil Eckoldt Waffenfabrik of Suhl, Germany on rifles, 1923-39.

ECLIPSE — Tradename on pistols made by Johnson, Bye & Co., ca. 1875.

edg — WW-II German ordnance code assigned to J.A. Henckels, Zwillingswerke, Solingen, Germany.

edk — WW-II German ordnance code assigned to Auto-Union, Zschoppau plant, Saxony.

edq — Deutsche Waffen- U. Munitionswerke AG, Lubeck-Schlutrup, Germany.

eds — WW-II German ordnance code assigned to Zundapp, Nurnberg, Germany.

eed — WW-II German ordnance code assigned to Gewehr- U. Fahrradteilfabrik H. Weirach, Zella-Mehlis, Germany.

eeg — WW-II German ordnance code assigned to Hermann Weirach, Gewehr- u. Fahrradteilfabrik.

eej — WW-II German ordnance code assigned to Markisches Walzwerk, Stausgberg, district Potsdam, Germany.

eel — WW-II German ordnance code assigned to Metallwarenfabrik Wissner.

eem — WW-II German ordnance code assigned to Selve-Kornbiegel, Dornheim AG, Munitionsfabrik.

eeo — WW-II German ordnance code assigned to Deutsche Waffen- u. Munitionsfabriken AG, Posen plant.

eey — WW-II German ordnance code assigned to Metallwarenfabrik Treuenfrietzen GmbH, Roderhof plant.

egy — WW-II German ordnance code assigned to Ing. Fr. August Pfeffer, Oberlind, Thuringia.

EIG — Importers of small pistols and revolvers in Miami, Fla. about 1967.

84 GUN CO. — Importer of sporting arms in Eighty-Four, Pa., ca. 1973.

eky — WW-II German ordnance code assigned to Volkswagenwerk, Wolfsburg.

EL CANO — Tradename used by Arana y Cia. on revolvers.

EL CID — Tradename of Casmiro Santos on pistols.

ELDORADO — Tradename on shotguns imported from Spain by Hy-Score Arms Corp.

ELECTOR — Tradename on revolvers made by Hopkins & Allen, ca. 1880.

ELECTRIC — Tradename on revolvers made by Forehand & Wadsworth, ca. 1880.

ELECTRIQUE — Tradename used on electrically fired guns made by SMFM, ca. 1965.

ELECTROARM — Tradename on electric free pistols made by Independent Research & Development, Inc. of San Antonio, Tex., ca. 1971.

11.25M/M AUT. PISTOL M/1914 — Marking on .45 acp Colt M1911 pistol copy made by Kongsberg Vapenfabriks, in Kongsberg, Norway.

elg — WW-II German ordnance code assigned to WASAG, Elsnig plant.

EL GAMO — Tradename on sporting arms made near Barcelona, Spain since about 1970.

ELGIN ARMS CO. — Tradename of Fred Bifflar & Co. of Chicago, Ill. on shotguns made by Crescent Fire Arms Co.

ELITE — Tradename of Mre. d'Armes des Pyrenees on pistols.

ELLUNAR LEBEL RAPIDE — Tradename used on revolvers by Garate, Anitua y Cia.

EL PERRO — Tradename of Lascurarin y Olasolo of Eibar, Spain on pistols.

E.M.F. — Abbreviation and tradename for Early and Modern Firearms Corp., a current manufacturer and importer of blackpowder and cartridge arms in Studio City, Calif.

EM-GE — Tradename used on revolvers by Gerstenberger & Eberwein.

emp — WW-II German ordnance code assigned to Dynamit AG (Alfred Nobel & Co.), Empelde plant.

EMPIRE — Tradename on spur trigger revolvers made by Jacob Rupertus, ca. 1880.

EMPIRE ARMS — Tradename on revolvers made by Meriden Arms Co. and distributed by H & D Folsom.

EMPIRE ARMS CO. — Tradename on shotguns made for Sears, Roebuck & Co. by Crescent Fire Arms Co.

EMPIRE STATE — Tradename used by H & D Folsom on revolvers made by Meriden Firearms Co.

EMPRESS — Tradename used by Jacob Rupertus on revolvers, ca. 1880.

emq — WW-II German ordnance code assigned to Karl Zeiss, Jena.

emu — WW-II German ordnance code assigned to Mathe Uhrenfabrik, Schwenningen, Germany.

ENDERS OAKLEAF — Tradename used by Shapleigh Hardware Co. of St. Louis, Mo. on shotguns made by Crescent Fire Arms Co.

ENDERS ROYAL SERVICE — Tradename used by Shapleigh Hardware Co. of St. Louis, Mo. on shotguns made by Crescent Fire Arms Co.

ENFORCER — Tradename and model designation of Universal Sporting Goods on M-1 carbine pistol.

ENTERPRISE — Tradename on revolvers made by the Enterprise Gun Works, Pittsburgh, Pa., ca. 1875.

enz — WW-II German ordnance code assigned to Enzesfelder Metallwerk, Enzesfeld plant, Vienna, Austria.

eom — WW-II German ordnance code assigned to H. Huck, Metallwarenfabrik, Nurnberg, Germany.

eqf — WW-II German ordnance code assigned to Karl Bocker, Lederwarenfabrik, Waldbrohl, Rheinland, Germany.

ERA — Tradename used by F.I.E. on shotguns.

erg — WW-II German ordnance code assigned to A. Doppert, Treibriemenfabrik, Kitzingen.

ERIKA — Tradename of Firma Pfannl on pistols.

ERMA — Tradename of Erfurter Maschinen u. Werkzeugfabrik of Erfurt, Germany prior to WW II, now Erma-Werke of Dachua, West Germany.

ESMIT — Tradename used by Hijos de Juan Arrizabalaga of Eibar, Spain on revolvers.

eso — WW-II German ordnance code assigned to Optische Werke G. Rodenstock, Munich, Germany.

ESPECIAL — Tradename of Hijos de C. Arrizabalaga on pistols.

ESPERANZA Y UNCETA — See Astra.

ESSEX — Tradename used by Belknap Hardware Co. of Louisville, Ky. on shotguns made by Crescent Fire Arms Co.

ESSEX — Tradename used by J. Stevens Arms Co. on rifles and shotguns.

ESSEX ARMS CORP. — Manufacturers of M1911 type pistols and frames since 1970 in Island Pond, Vt.

ESTRELLA — Tradename of Bonifacio Echeverria on pistols.

etb — WW-II German ordnance code assigned to Steubing & Co., Graslitz, Sudeten, Germany.

ETNA — Tradename of Santigo Salaberrin of Ermua, Spain on pistols.

ETXEZARRAGA Y ABAITUA — Pistol manufacturers in Eibar, Spain, ca. 1925.

eue — WW-II German ordnance code assigned to Otto Reichel, Inh. Rudolf Fischer, Lederwarenfabrik, Lengfeld, Erzgebirge.

eug — WW-II German ordnance code assigned to Optische Prazisionswerke GmbH, Warsaw, Poland.

EUSARO — Tradename on revolvers from Esprin Hermanos.

ews — WW-II German ordnance code assigned to Skodawerke, Konigsgratz plant, Czechoslovakia.

ewx — WW-II German ordnance code assigned to Franz u. Karl Vogels, Lederwarenfabrik, Cologne, Germany.

EXCAM — Current importers in Hialeah, Fla.

EXCEL — Tradename used by Iver Johnson.

EXCELSIOR — Tradename on revolvers from Norwich Falls Pistol Co., ca. 1880.

exd — WW-II German ordnance code assigned to Auto-Union, Audi Plant.

exp — WW-II German ordnance code assigned to Hans Kollmorgen, Optische Anstalt, Berlin, Germany.

EXPERT RIFLE — Tradename used by Witte Hardware Co. of St. Louis, Mo.

EXPRESS — Tradename on revolvers made by Bacon Arms Co., ca. 1880.

EXPRESS — Tradename used by Tomas de Urizar y Cia. on pistols.

exs — WW-II German ordnance code assigned to Skodawerke, Koniggratz, Czechoslovakia.

exw — WW-II German ordnance code assigned to Metallwerke Holleischen, Kreis Mies, Sudeten Germany.

F

fa — WW-II German ordnance code assigned to Mansfeld AG, Hettstedt, Sudharz, Germany.

F.A. — Abbreviation for Francisco Arizmendi on handguns.

faa — WW-II German ordnance code assigned to Deutsche Waffen- u. Munitionsfabriken AG, Karlsruhe, Germany.

F.A.B. — Tradename used by Rohm on revolvers.

FAB. DE ARMAS ZARAGOZA — Maker of "Corla" pistols in Zaragoza, Mexico.

FABRICA NACIONAL DE ARMAS MEXICO — Manufacturer of military arms in Mexico City from about 1923. Maker of Obregon pistols.

FABRIQUE NATIONAL D'ARMES DE GUERRE — See F.N.

F.A.G. — Abbreviation for F. Arizmendi y Goenaga of Eibar, Spain.

FAL — Abbreviation for Fusil Automatique Legere, a rifle made by, or under license from, F.N.

FALCON — Tradename used on pistols by the SPESCO Corp. on .25's imported from West Germany.

FALCON — Tradename used by Astra-Unceta y Cia. on the Model 4000 pistol, calibers 9mm and 7.65 Parabellum.

FALCON — Tradename used by American Import Co. of San Francisco, Calif. on shotguns imported from Spain.

FALLING BLOCK WORKS — Manufacturer of single shot rifle actions in Troy, Mich., ca. 1972.

FAMAE — Tradename of Fab. de Material de Guerra del Ejercito of Santiago, Chile on pistols.

FAR — Tradename of Soc. Anon. des Fab. D'Armes Reunies on pistols.

FAST — Tradename of Echave, Arizmendi y Cia. on pistols.

FABRIQUE D'ARMES UNIES DE LIEGE — Manufacturer of pistols in Liege, Belgium 1923-28.

FARROW ARMS CO. — Manufacturer of rifles starting in Holyoke, Mass. in 1886, then moving to Memphis, Tenn. in 1890, Mason, Tenn. in 1891, Washington, D.C. in 1896, and West Palm Beach, Fla. in 1910 until about 1930.

FARWELL ARMS CO. — Tradename used by Farwell, Ozmun, Kirk & Co. of St. Paul, Minn.

FAULTLESS — Tradename on shotguns used by John M. Smythe Hdw. Co. of Chicago, Ill. made by Crescent Fire Arms Co.

FAULTLESS GOOSE GUN — Tradename on shotguns used by John M. Smythe Hdw. Co. of Chicago, Ill., made by Crescent Fire Arms Co.

FAVORITE — Tradename on revolvers from Johnson, Bye & Co., ca. 1875.

FAVORITE NAVY — Tradename on revolvers made by Johnson, Bye & Co., ca. 1875.

fb — WW-II German ordnance code assigned to Mansfeld AG, Rothenburg plant, Saale, Germany.

FB — Abbreviation for the model "Frommer Baby" pistol made by Fegyver es Gepgyar Reszvenytarsasag.

FB — Abbreviation for Fabryka Broni on Radom pistols.

F.B.W. — Abbreviation for Falling Block Works on single shot rifles made in Troy, Mich., ca. 1972.

fc — WW-II German ordnance code assigned to Mansfeld AG, Alstedt plant, Thuringia, Germany.

fco — WW-II German ordnance code assigned to Sendlinger Optische Glaswerke GmbH, Berlin-Zehlendorf, Germany.

fd — WW-II German ordnance code assigned to Stolberger Metallwerke AG (Asten, Lynen & Shcleicher), Stolberg, Germany.

fde — WW-II German ordnance code assigned to Dynamit AG (Alfred Nobel & Co.), Forde plant.

FEDERAL ARMS — Tradename used by Sears, Roebuck & Co. on revolvers made by Meriden Firearms Co.

FEDERAL ORDNANCE — Importer and distributor in South El Monte, Calif.

FED ORD — Tradename of Federal Ordnance.

fee — WW-II German ordnance code assigned to Augsburger Waagenfabrik, Ludwig Pfisterer, Augsburg.

FEMARU — Femaru Fegyver-es Gepyar, manufacturer of Hungarian military pistols.

fer — WW-II German ordnance code assigned to Metallwerke Wandhofen, Schwerte, Westphalia, Germany.

FERLACH — City in Austria and tradename used by that city's gunmakers, the Genossenschaft der Buchsenmachermeister.

FERUNION — Current export house handling arms made in Hungary, located in Budapest.

F.I. — Abbreviation of Firearms International.

F.I.E. — Abbreviation and tradename for Firearms Import and Export Corp. in current operation in Miami, Fla. Manufacturers and distributors of both cartridge and blackpowder arms.

FIEL — Tradename of Erquiaga, Maguruza y Cia. on handguns.

FINLANDIA FIREARMS — Importers of Tikka arms in Sherman Oaks, Calif., ca. 1969.

FINNISH LION — Tradename on target rifles made by Valmet of Finland.

FIREARMS CENTER, INC. — Importers since about 1971 in Spokane, Wash.

FIREARMS INTERNATIONAL — Importers in Washington, D.C., taken over by Garcia Sporting Arms about 1970.

FIREARMS SPECIALTIES — Manufacturer of 45/70 revolvers in Owosso, Mich., ca. 1972.

fkx — WW-II German ordnance code assigned to Gustav Sudbrack, Lederwaren u. Gamaschenfabrik, Bielefeld.

F.L. SELBSTLADER — Tradename of Fritz Langenhan on pistols.

F.M.A.P. — Abbreviation for Fabrica Militar de Armas Portatiles of Rosario, Argentina on pistols.

F.M.G. — Abbreviation for Fab. de Material de Guerra Ejercito of Santiago, Chile on pistols.

F.N. — Abbreviation for Fabrique National d'Arms de Guerre, Herstal, Belgium from 1889 to date. Manufacturers of sporting and military arms, primarily known for its Browning designed weapons, and in the U.S. for guns labeled "Browning."

fnh — WW-II German ordnance code assigned to Bohmische Waffenfabrik, Strkonitz plant, Prague, Czechoslovakia.

FORBES, F.F. — Tradename used by H & D Folsom on shotguns made by Crescent Fire Arms Co.

FORENADE FAVRIK VERKEN — See FFV.

FOREVER YOURS — Tradename on shotguns imported by Flaig's Lodge, Millvale, Pa.

FORJAS TAURUS S.A. — Current manufacturer of revolvers in P. Alegre, Brazil under the tradename "Taurus."

FOSTER, JAS. H. & CO. — Tradename on shotguns made by F.J. Abbey & Co. of Chicago, Ill., ca. 1878.

FORTUNA — Tradename of Unceta y Cia. (Astra) on pistols.

FORTUNA WERKE — Current manufacturer of sporting arms in Suhl, East Germany.

42 — WW-II German ordnance code assigned to Mauser-Werke, Oberndorf am Neckar, Germany. Some authorities claim that up until 1937 this code was used by Simson & Co. of Suhl, Germany, but this is unproven.

480 — WW-II German ordnance code assigned to Carl Walther, Zella-Mehlis, Germany.

FOX — Tradename of Ceska Zbrojovka on pistols.

fpx — WW-II German ordnance code assigned to Schaffer & Budenberg, Magdeburg-Buckau, Germany.

fqn — WW-II German ordnance code assigned to Vereinigte Leichtmetallwerke, Hannover-Linden, Germany.

fra — WW-II German ordnance code assigned to Draht- und Metallwarenfabrik GmbH, Salzwedel.

FRANCAISE — Tradename of Mre. d'Armes Automatiques Francaise, not to be confused with Le Francaise.

FRANKLIN, C.W. — Tradename used by H & D Folsom on shotguns imported from Belgium.

FRANZ STOCK — See STOCK, FRANZ.

FRATELLI GAMBA — Current manufacturer of sporting arms in Brescia, Italy.

FREELAND, AL — Current importer in Rock Island, Ill. of target arms.

FROMMER — Tradename of Fegyveres Gepygar Reszvenytarsasag, later Femaru Fegyver-es Gepyar on pistols.

FRONTIER — Tradename used on revolvers made by Norwich Falls Pistol Co., ca. 1880.

FRONTIER BULLDOG — Tradename on revolvers from Fabrique National d'Armes de Guerre (Belgium).

FRONTIER BULLDOG — Tradename on revolvers from Fab. d'Armes de Guerre.

FRONTIER DERRINGER — Tradename used by Hy Hunter of Burbank, Calif., ca. 1960.

frp — WW-II German ordnance code assigned to Stahlwerke Harkot-Eicken, Hagen, Westphalia, Germany.

FRYBERG, ANDREW & CO. — Revolver maker in Hopkintown, Mass., ca. 1905.

FS — Abbreviation on grips for the model "Frommer Stop" pistol made by Fegyver es Gepgyar Esszvenytarsasag.

fsx — WW-II German ordnance code assigned to Albin Scholle, Lederwarenfabrik, Zeitz.

ftc — WW-II German ordnance code assigned to Frost & Jahnel, Breslau, Czechoslovakia.

fue — WW-II German ordnance code assigned to Skodawerke, machine shop, Dubnica plant, Czechoslovakia.

FUJISEIKI SEISAKUSHO CO. LTD. — Shotgun manufacturer in Okazaki City, Japan.

FUROR — Tradename of Mre. d'Armes des Pyrenees on pistols.

FURTSCHEGGER — Manufacturer of sporting arms in Kufstein, Austria, currently making arms for Waffen Frankonia.

FURY — Tradename used by L.A. Distributors, ca. 1969 on pistols.

fuu — WW-II German ordnance code assigned to Strube GmbH, subsidiary of Polte, Magdeburg, Germany.

fva — WW-II German ordnance code assigned to Draht- u. Metallwarenfabrik GmbH, Salzwedel.

fwh — WW-II German ordnance code assigned to Norddreutsche Maschinenfabrik GmbH, main office, Berlin, Germany.

fwr — WW-II German ordnance code assigned to Optische Anstalt Saalfeld GmbH, Saalfeld.

fwz — WW-II German ordnance code assigned to Eisen- u. Emaillierwerke Wilhelmshutte, Sprottau-Wilhelmshutte.

fxa — WW-II German ordnance code assigned to Eisenacher Karosseriewerk Assman GmbH, Eisenach.

fxo — WW-II German ordnance code assigned to C.G. Haenel, Waffen- u. Fahrradfabrik, Suhl, Germany.

fxp — WW-II German ordnance code assigned to Hans Kollmorgen, Optische Anstalt, Berlin.

fyd — WW-II German ordnance code assigned to Skodawerke, Adamsthal plant.

fze — WW-II German ordnance code assigned to Waffenfabrik Holler, Solingen, Germany.

fzs — WW-II German ordnance code assigned to Waffenfabrik Heinrich Krieghoff, Suhl, Germany.

G

ga — WW-II German ordnance code assigned to Hirsch, Kupfer- u. Messingwerk AG, Finow.

G.A.C. FIREARMS MFG. CO. — Tradename on Spanish revolvers possibly referring to Garate-Anitua Cia.

GALEF, J. L. & SON — Current importer of sporting arms in N.Y.C.

GALESI — Tradename for Industria Armi Galesi on pistols.

GALLIA — Purported to be tradename of Mre. d'Armes des Pyrenees on pistols.

GALLUS — Tradename of Retolaza Hermanos of Eibar, Spain on pistols.

GAMBA, RENATO — Sporting arms manufacturer in Brescia, Italy since 1974.

GAME GETTER — Tradename of Marble Arms & Mfg. Co., ca. 1908.

gaq — WW-II German ordnance code assigned to Otto Stephan, Leder- u. Lederwarenfabrik, Muhlhausen.

GARRISON — Tradename of revolvers made by Hopkins & Allen, ca. 1880.

GARRUCHA — Tradename on double-barrel pistols made by Amadeo Rossi of Sao Leopoldo, Brazil.

gau — WW-II German ordnance code assigned to Sudhaus & Sohne, Iserlohn.

GAULOIS — Tradename of Mre. Francaise d'Armes et Cycles de St. Etienne on pistols.

gb — WW-II German ordnance code assigned to Vereinigte N. Werke, Schwerte

gbv — WW-II German ordnance code assigned to Witte & Co., Velbert.

gcw — WW-II German ordnance code assigned to Gohring-hebenstreit, Radebeul near Dresden, Germany.

gcx — WW-II German ordnance code assigned to Karl Brettschneider, Mahr.-Schonberg.

GEBR. MAUSER ET CIE. — See Mauser Werke Ag.

GEBRUDER REMPT — Manufacturer of sporting arms in Suhl, Germany from 1865 to about 1940. Best known for "Remo" rifles.

GECADO — Tradename of G.C. Dornheim, Suhl, Germany.

GECO — Tradename of August Genschow.

G & E — Abbreviation for Gerstenberger & Eberwein on revolvers.

GEM — Tradename used on pistols, ca. 1870 marketed by Stevens Arms & Tool Co., and possibly made by them. This name is also attributed to Iver Johnson and Bacon Mfg. Co.

GERATE MENDIBE — Post-WW-II manufacturer of sporting arms in Eibar, Spain.

GERING, H.M. — Pistol maker in the early 1920's in Arnstadt, Germany; made Leonhardt pistols.

GERSTENBERGER & EBERWEIN — Manufacturer of handguns in Gussenstadt, West Germany.

geu — WW-II German ordnance code assigned to Juhbier & Co., Prazisionspresgtucke, Wipperfurth.

GEVARM — Tradename used by Gevelot in Paris, France.

gfg — WW-II German ordnance code assigned to Karl Hepting & Co., Leder- u. Gurtelfabrik, Stuttgart, Germany.

ggb — WW-II German ordnance code assigned to I.G. Konigshutte u. Laurahutte Kattowatz, main office, Rochling, Konigshutte.

G.H. — Abbreviation for Guisasola Hermanos of Eibar, Spain on revolvers.

G & H — Abbreviation for Griffen & Howe.

ghf — WW-II German ordnance code assigned to Fritz Kiess & Co., GmbH, Waffenfabrik, Suhl, Germany.

ghp — WW-II German ordnance code assigned to Ruf & Co., Optische Werke Kassel, Hessen-Nassau, Germany.

GIBRALTER — Tradename of Sears, Roebuck & Co. on revolvers probably made by Meriden Firearms Co.

gil — WW-II German ordnance code assigned to Auto-Union, Spandau plant, Germany.

gjh — WW-II German ordnance code assigned to Rudolph Conte, Nachf. Theodor Seibold, Fabrik fur Lederwaren, Offenbach am, Germany.

gk — WW-II German ordnance code assigned to Mansfeld AG, Hettstedt, Sudharz.

GLADIATOR — Tradename used by Sears, Roebuck & Co.

GLASER, W. WAFFEN — Manufacturer, importer, and distributor in Zurich, Switzerland since 1866.

GLENFIELD — Tradename of Marlin Firearms, in current production.

GLORIA — Tradename of Gregorio Bolumburu of Eibar, Spain on pistols.

G.M. — Abbreviation on sporting arms made in Eibar, Spain by Gerate Mendibe & Co., post-WW-II.

gmo — WW-II German ordnance code assigned to Rahm & Kampmann, Lederwarenfabrik, Kaiserslautern plant.

gn — WW-II German ordnance code assigned to Aug. Wellner, Aue, Saxony.

GOLDEN EAGLE — Tradename used on arms made in Japan by Nikko Arms Co. Ltd.

GOLD RUSH — Tradename on derringers imported by Hy Hunter of Burbank, Calif., ca. 1960.

GOLIAT — Tradename on revolvers from Antonio Errasti.

GOOSE GUN — Tradename on shotguns from J. Stevens Arms Co.

GRANT HAMMOND MFG. CORP. — New Haven, Conn. 1915-17, auto pistol maker.

GRANT, STEVEN & SONS — Manufacturer of sporting arms in London, England 1841 until merger with Charles Lancaster & Co. and Lang & Hussey to form Joseph Lang & Co.

GRANT, W.L. — Tradename on revolvers made by D.D. Cone.

GREAT WESTERN GUN WORKS — Distributors, importers and manufacturers of firearms from 1865 to about 1920 in Pittsburgh, Pa.

GREENFIELD — Tradename used by Hibbard, Spencer, Bartlett Co. of Chicago, Ill.

GREY EAGLE — Tradename used by American Import Co. on shotguns made in Italy by Zoli.

GREY EAGLE — Tradename used by American Import Co. on shotguns made in U.S.S.R.

GREYHAWK ARMS CORP. — South El Monte, Calif. Makers of single shot rifles, ca. 1975.

GRIFFEN & HOWE — Custom gunmakers in N.Y.C. from 1923. Absorbed by Abercrombie & Fitch in 1930.

GROSS ARMS CO. — Revolver maker in Tiffin, Ohio 1862-65.

grz — WW-II German ordnance code assigned to Gebr. Kruger, Lederwarenfabrik, Breslau, Czechoslovakia.

gsb — WW-II German ordnance code assigned to Rheinmetall-Borsig, branch-office Liege, operated by Loewen (S.A. des Ateliers de la Dyle), Belgium.

gsc — WW-II German ordnance code assigned to S.A. Belge des Mecanique et de L'Armement, Monceau-sur-Sambre, Belgium.

gtb — WW-II German ordnance code assigned to J.F. Eisfeld GmbH, Pulver- u. Pyrotechnische Fabriken, Guntersberge plant.

GUARDIAN — Tradename on revolvers made by Bacon Arms Co., ca. 1880.

GUARDIAN — Tradename used on revolvers by F.I.E., ca. 1970.

gug — WW-II German ordnance code assigned to Ungarische Optische Werke AG, Budapest, Hungary.

guj — WW-II German ordnance code assigned to Werner D. Kuhn, Optische Industrie, Berlin-Steglitz, Germany.

gum — WW-II German ordnance code assigned to Bergisch-Markische Eisenwerke, Velbert, Rheinland, Germany.

GUNTHER, S. — Pre-WW-II manufacturer of sporting arms in Suhl, Germany.

GUSTLOFF-WERKE — Manufacturer of pistols and military arms in Suhl, Germany from about 1938 to 1945.

gut — WW-II German ordnance code assigned to Walter Schurmann & Co., Lederwarenfabrik, Bielefeld.

guy — WW-II German ordnance code assigned to Werkzeugmaschinenfabrik Oelikon, Buhrle & Co., Zurich, Switzerland.

gvj — WW-II German ordnance code assigned to Ruhrstahl AG, Gelsenkirchen.

gxy — WW-II German ordnance code assigned to Klinge, Lederwarenfabrik, Dresden-Lobtau, Germany.

gyf — WW-II German ordnance code assigned to DEW, Bochum plant.

gyo — WW-II German ordnance code assigned to Hans Dinkelmaeyer, Lederwarenfabrik, Nurnberg, Germany.

GYOSELEM — Tradename on rifles from Ferunion.

gzf — WW-II German ordnance code assigned to Westfalische Eisen- u. Bleckwarenwerke, Siegen, Germany.

H

ha — WW-II German ordnance code assigned to Treuenbrietzen Metallwarenfabrik GmbH, Sebaldushof plant.

H. & A. — Tradename and abbreviation for Hopkins & Allen.

HAENEL, C.G. WAFFEN UND FAHRRADFABRIK — Manufacturers of sporting and military firearms in Suhl, Germany from 1840 until 1945 when it became Ernst Thalman-Werk VEB.

HAENEL-Schmeisser — Tradename of C.G. Haenel Waffen und Fahrradfabrik.

HAERENS RUSTKAMMER — Marking on Bayard/Bergmann pistols made by Anciens Etablissments Pieper under Danish contract, mark means "Army Storage Arsenal."

HAERENS TØJHUS — Marking on Bayard/Bergmann pistols made by Anciens Etablissments Pieper under Danish contract. Mark means "Royal Army."

HAFDASA — Tradename of Hispano Argentina Fab. de Automoviles.

HALBE & GERLICH — Manufacturers of arms and ammunition in Hamburg, Germany from 1922.

HALCON — Tradename on .22 rifles of Metalurgica Centro in Argentina.

HALF-BREED — Tradename on revolvers made by Hopkins & Allen, ca. 1880.

HALGER — Tradename of Halbe & Gerlich of Hamburg, Germany.

ham — WW-II German ordnance code assigned to Dynamit AG (Alfred Nobel & Co.), Hamm plant.

HAMILTON — Tradename of Torssin & Son on pistols.

HAMILTON RIFLE CO. — Rifle maker in Plymouth, Mich. from about 1925 to 1932.

HAMMERLI — Lenzburg, Switzerland from about 1922 to date; makers of target firearms.

HANDY GUN — Tradename used by Harrington & Richardson on shotgun-pistols.

HANSCOMB HDW. CO. — Tradename used by company of the same name in Haverhill, Mass.

HARD PAN — Tradename on revolvers used by Hood Firearms Co., ca. 1875.

HARRINGTON & RICHARDSON — Gunmakers in Worcester, Mass. since 1874. Successors to Wesson & Harrington. Manufacturers of sporting and military arms now located in Gardner, Mass.

HARRISON ARMS CO. — Tradename used by Sickles & Preston of Davenport, Iowa on shotguns imported from Belgium.

HARTFORD ARMS & EQUIPMENT CO. — Manufacturer of handguns in Hartford, Conn. from 1929 until they were purchased by High Standard in 1932.

HARVARD — Tradename used by H & D Folsom on shotguns made by Crescent Fire Arms Co.

has — WW-II German ordnance code assigned to Pulverfabrik Hasloch, Hasloch on the Main, Germany.

HASAG — Tradename of Hugo Schneider, AG.

HAUCK, WILBUR J. — Manufacturer of single shot rifles in West Arlington, Vt., ca. 1950.

HAWES FIREARMS CO. — Current importers located in Van Nuys, Calif.

HAWES MARSHAL — Tradename on single action revolvers made for Hawes by J.P. Sauer & Sohn of West Germany.

hbg — WW-II German ordnance code assigned to Alfred Schwarz AG, Metallwerk Frodenburg on the Ruhr, Eisenach plant, Germany.

hbu — WW-II German ordnance code assigned to Heinrich List, Elektrotechnik u. Mechanik, Teltow & Steglitz.

hck — WW-II German ordnance code assigned to Georg A. Lerch GmbH, Lederwaren u. Stanzwerk, Mettman, Rheinland, Germany.

H & D — Abbreviation for Henrion & Dassy of Liege, Belgium, ca. 1900.

H.D.H. — Abbreviation for Henrion, Dassy et Heuschen of Liege, Belgium, ca. 1910.

hdt — WW-II German ordnance code assigned to Markischer Metallbau, Oranienburg.

hdv — WW-II German ordnance code assigned to Optische Werke Osterrode GmbH, Osterrode, Harz.

HEGE WAFFEN — Tradename on copies of Walther PP marketed in West Germany by Hebsacker Gesellschaft, and made by Fegyver es Gepgyar Resvenytarsasag in Budapest, Hungary.

HEGE WAFFEN — Tradename used by Hege GmbH & Co. of Schwabisch Hall, West Germany on sporting arms.

HEIM — Tradename of C.E. Heinzelmann on sporting arms.

HEINZELMANN, C.E. — Gunmaker in Plochingen, Wurtemberg, Germany 1921-28. Used the tradename "Heim."

HELFRICHT — Tradename of A. Krauser Waffenfabrik on pistols.

HELFRICHT & FISCHER — Manufacturers of sporting arms in Zella-

Mehlis, Germany from 1933 to 1940.

HELKRA — Tradename of A. Krauser Waffenfabrik on pistols.

HENRY GUN CO. — Tradename used on Belgian shotguns, ca. 1900.

HERCULES — Tradename used by J. Stevens Arms Co. on shotguns.

HERCULES — Tradename used by Montgomery Ward & Co. on arms made by Iver Johnson.

HERMETIC — Tradename of Bernardon-Martin on pistols.

HERMITAGE — Tradename used by the J. Stevens Arms Co. on their Model 90 shotgun.

HERMITAGE ARMS CO. — Tradename of Grey & Dudley Hdw. Co., Nashville, Tenn. on shotguns made by Crescent Fire Arms Co.

HERMITAGE GUN CO. — See Hermitage Arms Co.

HERO — Tradename on revolvers used by Tryon Bros. Co., made by Rupertus Arms Co., ca. 1880.

HEROLD — Tradename used on rifles and pistols by Franz Jager & Co. of Suhl, Germany, 1923-39.

HEROLD-REPETIERBUCHSE — Tradename used on rifles made by Franz Jager & Co. of Suhl, Germany from 1923-39.

HERTERS, INC. — Importers and distributors of firearms in Waseca, Minn.

hew — WW-II German ordnance code assigned to Ing. F. Janecek, Waffenwerke, Prague, Czechoslovakia.

HEYM, FRANZ W. — Manufacturer of sporting arms in Suhl, Germany from 1934 to 1945, now located in Munnerstadt, West Germany.

HEYM GEBRUDER — Manufacturers of sporting arms in Suhl, Germany 1922-39.

HEYM, MAX — Manufacturer of sporting arms in Suhl, Germany 1934-39.

hft — WW-II German ordnance code assigned to Becker & Co., GmbH, Militar- u. Feuerwehrausrustungen, Berlin, Germany.

hgs — WW-II German ordnance code assigned to W. Gustav Burmeister, Pyrotechnische Fabrik u. Signalmittelwerk (fireworks and pyrotechnics), Hamburg.

H & H — Tradename and abbreviation for Holland & Holland.

hhc — WW-II German ordnance code assigned to Union Gesellschaft f. Metallindustrie, Sils van de Loo & Co., Frodenberg plant.

hhg — WW-II German ordnance code assigned to Rheinmetall-Borsig AG, Tegel plant.

hhu — WW-II German ordnance code assigned to Metallwarenfabrik Schmalkalden.

hhv — WW-II German ordnance code assigned to Steyr-Daimler-Puch AG, Nibelungen plant, St. Valentin, Austria.

hhw — WW-II German ordnance code assigned to Metallwerke Silberhutte GmbH, Andreasberg, Harz.

hhz — WW-II German ordnance code assigned to Rochlingwerke, Volklingen.

HIB SPE BAR — Abbreviation and tradename used by Hibbard, Spencer, Bartlett Co. of Chicago, Ill.

HIGGINS, J.C. — Tradename of Sears, Roebuck & Co. for firearms made by various manufacturers.

HIJO — Tradename of Industri Armi Galesi on pistols.

HI-SHEAR CORP. — Manufacturer of the "Omega" rifle, currently located in Torrence, Calif.

hjg — WW-II German ordnance code assigned to Kimmach & Brunn, Fabrik fur Heeresausrustung, Kaiserslautern.

hjh — WW-II German ordnance code assigned to Karl Ackva, Lederfabrik, Bad Kreuznach.

H.K. — Abbreviation for Heckler & Koch.

hkm — WW-II German ordnance code assigned to Karl Braun AG, Optische Industrie, Nurnberg.

hla — WW-II German ordnance code assigned to Metallwarenfabrik Treuenbrietzen GmbH, Sebalddushof plant.

hlb — WW-II German ordnance code assigned to Metallwarenfabrik Treuenbrietzen GmbH, Selterhof plant.

hlc — WW-II German ordnance code assigned to Zieh- u. Stanzwerk (wire pulling and stamping), Schleusingen.

hld — WW-II German ordnance code assigned to Metallwarenfabrik Treuenbrietzen GmbH, Belsig plant.

hle — WW-II German ordnance code assigned to Metallwarenfabrik Treuenbrietzen GmbH, Roderhof plant.

hlv — WW-II German ordnance code assigned to Maury & Co., Lederwarenfabrik, Offenbach on the Main.

H & N — MINICRAFT, INC. — Manufacturer of the Thomas pistol in Covina, Calif.

hnx — WW-II German ordnance code assigned to Walter KG, Kiel, Kiel plant and Tannenberg plant.

HOFFMAN ARMS CO. — Cleveland, Ohio, ca. 1925, makers of custom rifles.

HOLDEN, CYRUS B. — Manufacturer of rifles in Worcester, Mass. 1864 possibly until 1880.

HOLLAND & HOLLAND — London, England from 1835, manufacturers of fine sporting arms.

HOLLENBECK, F.A. — Manufacturer of repeating rifles in Syracuse, N.Y. 1910-11.

HOLT, SAM — Tradename used by Sears, Roebuck & Co. on shotguns.

HOPKINS & ALLEN — Established in Norwich, Conn. in 1868, taken over by Marlin-Rockwell in 1917, and now owned by Numrich Arms Corp. and located in West Hurley, N.Y. Manufacturers of all types of sporting arms, but best known for their early revolvers.

HOPKINS, C.W. — Tradename used

by Bacon Arms Co., ca. 1875 on revolvers.

HOWA MACHINERY, LTD. — Manufacturer of sporting and military arms in Nagoya, Japan since 1940.

HOWARD ARMS CO. — Tradename on shotguns used by Fred Bifflar & Co. of Chicago, Ill., made by Crescent Fire Arms Co.

HOWARD ARMS CO. — Tradename used by Meriden Firearms Co. on revolvers.

H & R — Abbreviation and tradename for Harrington & Richardson.

hrn — WW-II German ordnance code assigned to Presswerk Metgethen, East Prussia.

H.S. — Abbreviation for High Standard on American made firearms, and for Herbert Schmidt on revolvers made in West Germany.

H.S.B. & CO. — Abbreviation for Hibbard, Spencer, Bartlett & Co. of Chicago, Ill., distributors of private-label arms from various makers.

htg — WW-II German ordnance code assigned to Polte Armaturen- u. Maschinenfabriken AG, Duderstadt plant, Westphalia.

htq — WW-II German ordnance code assigned to Junghanswerke, Schwenningen plant.

HUBERTUS — Tradename of Imman, Meffert Gewehrfabrik, Suhl, Germany on sporting arms, 1839-1945.

HUDSON — Tradename used by Hibbard, Spencer, Bartlett Co. of Chicago, Ill.

HUMMER — Tradename used by Lee Hardware of Salina, Kansas on shotguns imported from Belgium.

HUNTER ARMS CO. — Shotgun manufacturer who purchased the L.C. Smith Gun Co. of Syracuse, N.Y. in 1890, and continued to make the L.C. Smith shotgun, along with "Hunter" and "Fulton" branded guns. Located in Fulton, N.Y., they were taken over by Marlin Firearms in 1948.

HUSKY — Tradename used by Tradewinds of Tacoma, Wash. on Husqvarna rifles.

HUSQVARNA — Tradename for Husqvarna Vapenfabrik Akiebolag, makers of a wide range of firearms since 1867 in Jonkoping, Sweden.

H.V. — Abbreviation for Hourat et Vie. on pistols.

HVA — Abbreviation and tradename for Husqvarna Vapenfabrik Akitiebolag.

HW — Abbreviation and tradename of Herman Weihrauch Sportwaffenfabrik on revolvers made in West Germany.

hwd — WW-II German ordnance code assigned to Westfalische-Anhaltische Sprengstoff AG, Herrenwald plant.

H. W-Z — Abbreviation for Hersteller Weihrauch, sporting arms manufacturer in Zella-Mehlis, Germany 1934-38.

HY HUNTER CORP. — Importer and dealer in Hollywood, Calif. in the mid-1950's.

HYPER-SINGLE PRECISION SS RIFLES — Current manufacturer of rifles in Jenks, Okla.

HY SCORE ARMS CO. — Importers in Brooklyn, N.Y. of sporting arms.

I

i — WW-II German ordnance code assigned to Astra-Werke, Chemnitz.

IAB — Tradename on shotguns made in Italy for Puccinelli of San Anselm, Calif.

IAB, SpA. — Current manufacturer of blackpowder and cartridge replica firearms in Marcheno, Italy.

I.A.G. — Abbreviation for Industria Armi Galesi on pistols.

I.B.M. — Abbreviation for International Business Machine, manufacturer of M-1 Carbines during WW-II at Poughkeepsie, N.Y.

IDEAL — Tradename used by Francisco Arizmendi on pistols.

ILLINOIS ARMS CO. — Tradename used by Friederich Pickert (Germany) on revolvers.

I.M.I. — Abbreviation for Israeli Military Industries Tel Aviv, Israel.

IMPERIAL — Tradename on pistols for Tomas de Urizar y Cia.

IMPERIAL — Tradename on pistols used by Gregorio Bolumburu.

IMPERIAL ARMS — Tradename on revolvers from Hopkins & Allen, ca. 1880.

I.N.A. — Abbreviation for Industria National de Armas, Sao Paulo, Brazil.

INDEPENDENT RESEARCH & DEVELOPMENT, INC. — Manufacturer of electrically-fired free pistols in San Antonio, Tex., ca. 1971.

INDIAN — Tradename on pistols used by Isidro Gaztanaga.

INDIAN ARMS CORP. — Current manufacturer of pistols in Detroit, Mich.

INDUNA — Tradename of Industrial Units (Pty) Ltd. of Johannesburg, South Africa.

INDUSTRIA ARMI GALESI — Manufacturer of pistols in Collebeato, Italy since 1910.

INDUSTRIA NACIONAL DE ARMAS — Government arms plant in Sao Paulo, Brazil.

INFALLIBLE — Tradename on pistols manufactured by the Warner Arms Corp.

INGLIS, JOHN CO. — WW-II manufacturer of Browning Model 1935 9mm pistols in Toronto, Canada under license from F.N.

INGRAM — Tradename on submachine guns made by Police Ordnance Co. of Los Angeles and Military Armament Corp. of Ga.

INHAUSER, CARL — Manufacturer of military arms in Vienna, Austria 1922-45.

INLAND — A division of General Motors in Dayton, Ohio that manufactured M-1 carbines during WW-II.

INTERARMCO — See Interarms.

INTERARMS — Importers and manufacturers of sporting arms since the mid-1950's in Alexandria, Va.

INTERCHANGEABLE — Tradename on shotguns used by Schoverlin-Daley & Gales for guns made in Belgium, ca. 1880.

INTERNATIONAL — Tradename used by E.C. Meacham of St. Louis, Mo. on revolvers made by Hood Firearms, ca. 1880.

INTERSTATE ARMS CO. — Tradename on shotguns used by Townley Metal & Hdw., Kansas City, Mo., made by Crescent Fire Arms Co.

INVICTA — Tradename on pistols used by Santigo Salaberrin.

IRIS — Tradename used by Orbea Hermanos.

IROQUOIS — Tradename used by Remington Arms Co. on revolvers.

IRWIN-PEDERSEN — Manufacturer of M-1 carbines during WW-II in Grand Rapids, Mich.

ISHAPORE — Government small arms plant in India.

ITALGUNS INTERNATIONAL — Current manufacturer of sporting arms in Cusago, Italy.

ITHACA GUN CO. — Manufacturer of sporting arms in Ithaca, N.Y. since 1873. In 1904 they incorporated and between 1908 and 1926 they absorbed Lefever Arms Co., Wilkes Barre Gun Co., Union Firearms Co., and Syracuse Arms Co.

IVER JOHNSON ARMS & CYCLE WORKS — Manufacturer of sporting arms since it started as Johnson, Bye & Co. in 1871 at Worcester, Mass. In 1883 became Iver Johnson & Co., and was again changed to its current form in 1884. In 1891 the firm moved to Finchburg, Mass.

IXOR — Tradename of Mre. d'Armes des Pyrenees on pistols.

IZARRA — Tradename used by Bonafacio Echevarria.

J

ja — WW-II German ordnance code assigned to Schmole, Menden.

JACKRABBIT — Tradename used by Continental Arms on convertible .44/.410 pistol with shoulder stock, ca. 1960.

JACKSON ARMS CO. — Tradename used by C.M. McClung & Co. of Knoxville, Tenn. on shotguns made by Crescent Fire Arms Co.

JACKSON HOLE RIFLE CO. — Manufacturer of Take-down rifles in Jackson Hole, Wyo., ca. 1970.

JAGA — Tradename used by Frantisek Dusek on pistols made in Czechoslovakia.

JAGER, FRANZ & CO. — Gunmakers in Suhl, Germany from 1923 to 1939.

jan — WW-II German ordnance code assigned to Deutsche Versuchsanstalt fur Luftfahrt, Berlin-Adlerhof.

JANA INTERNATIONAL CO. — Current importers of sporting arms in Denver, Colo.

JANCCEK, F. — Small arms maker in Reichenberg and Praha, Czechoslovakia 1930-39.

JANSSEN FRERES — Sporting arms manufacturers in Liege, Belgium 1925-39.

jba — WW-II German ordnance code assigned to A. Wunderlich Nachf., Fabrik fur Heeresausrustung (factory for military equipment), Berlin-Neukolln.

JEFFERSON — Tradename used by Kodiak Mfg. Co. of North Haven, Conn., ca. 1965.

JEFFERY, W. & SON — Revolver makers in Plymouth, England 1866-1929.

JEFFERY, W.J. & CO. — Manufacturer of military and sporting arms in London, England since 1888.

JENKINS SAFETY CATCH GUN CO. — Shotgun maker in Rock Hill, S.C., ca. 1893.

JEWEL — Tradename on revolvers from Hood Firearms Co., ca. 1875.

jfp — WW-II German ordnance code assigned to Dr. Karl Leiss, Optische Mechanische Instrumente, Berlin-Steglitz.

jfs — WW-II German ordnance code assigned to Junkers, Magdeburg division.

J.G.A. — Abbreviation and tradename of J.G. Anschutz Germaniawaffenfabrik on rifles and revolvers.

J.G.L. — Abbreviation for J.G. Landmann, manufacturer of rifles in West Germany, ca. 1968.

jhg — WW-II German ordnance code assigned to Gustav Genschow & Co., AG, Lederwarenfabriken, Alstadt-Hachenburg.

jhv — WW-II German ordnance code assigned to Metallwaren, Waffen- und Maschinenfabrik AG, Budapest, Hungary.

JIEFFECO — Tradename used by Robar et Cie.

JINSEN ARSENAL — Japanese small arms plant in Inchon, Korea during WW-II.

jkg — WW-II German ordnance code assigned to Konigl. Ungar. Staatliche Eisen-, Stahl- u. Maschinenfabrik, Budapest, Hungary.

J-K IMPORTS — Current importers in Novato, Calif.

jlj — WW-II German ordnance code assigned to HeeresZeugamt Ingolstadt.

jln — WW-II German ordnance code assigned to Deutsche Lederwerkstatten GmbH, Pirmasens, Germany.

J.M. — Tradename and abbreviation of Marlin Firearms Co.

J.M.M. — Tradename and abbreviation of J.M. Marlin.

jme — WW-II German ordnance code assigned to Armeemarinehaus Berlin, Berlin-Charlottenburg, Germany.

jnh — WW-II German ordnance code assigned to Hensoldt Werke fur Optik u. Mechanik, Herborn, Dillkreis, Germany.

J-9 — Tradename used by Herters on rifles made by Zavodi Crvena Zastava of Belgrade, Yugoslavia.

jnk — WW-II German ordnance code assigned to Conti, Hannover, Germany.

jnw — WW-II German ordnance code assigned to Eisenwerk Steele, Essen-Steele, Germany.

joa — WW-II German ordnance code assigned to Dresdner Koffer- u. Taschenfabrik, Karl Heinichen, Dresden, Germany.

JOHNSON, BYE & CO. — See Iver Johnson.

JOHNSTON-TUCKER FIREARMS — Manufacturer of M-1 carbine type rifles in St. Louis, Mo., ca. 1965.

JOKER — Tradename used by Hopkins & Allen on revolvers, ca. 1870.

JO-LO-AR — Tradename used by Hijos de Calixto Arrizabalaga.

jrr — WW-II German ordnance code assigned to Junghans, Renchen plant, Baden, Germany.

jrs — WW-II German ordnance code assigned to Junghans, branch office, Vienna, Austria.

jry — WW-II German ordnance code assigned to Hermann Herold, Olberhain, Germany.

jsd — WW-II German ordnance code assigned to Gustav Reinhard, Lederwarenfabrik, Berlin, Germany.

jse — WW-II German ordnance code assigned to Metallwerke Zoblitz AG, Zoblitz.

jtb — WW-II German ordnance code assigned to S.A. Tavaro, Ghent, Belgium.

jua — WW-II German ordnance code assigned to Danuvia Waffen- u. Munitionsfabriken AG, Budapest, Hungary.

JUBALA — Tradename used by Larranaga y Elartza.

JUNIOR — Tradename of Pretoria Arms Factory on pistols.

JUST, JOSEF — Manufacturer of sporting arms in Ferlach, Austria 1919-39.

jut — WW-II German ordnance code assigned to Vereinigte Wiener Metallwerke, Vienna, Austria.

jve — WW-II German ordnance code assigned to Optische Werke Ernst Ludwig, Weixdorf, Anhalt, Saxony, Germany.

jvf — WW-II German ordnance code assigned to Wilhelm Brand, Treibriemenfabrik, Heidelberg, Germany.

jwa — WW-II German ordnance code assigned to Moritz Stecher, Lederwerk, Freiburg, Germany, also: Manufacture Nationale d'Armes, Chatellerault, France.

jwh — WW-II German ordnance code assigned to Manufacture d'Armes, Chatellerault, Chatellerault, France.

K

k — WW-II German ordnance code assigned to Firma Luch & Wagner, Suhl, Germany.

ka — WW-II German ordnance code assigned to Gerhardi & Co., Ludenscheid, Westphalia, Germany.

KABA, KABA SPEZIAL — Tradenames of Karl Bauer, a Berlin, Germany dealer. Handguns made by Menz, August and Arizmendi, Francisco bear this name.

kam — WW-II German ordnance code assigned to Hasag, Eisen- u. Metallwerke GmbH, Skarzysko Kamienna.

KAYOBA FACTORY LTD. — Kayoba, Japan from about 1900 until taken over as part of Kokura Arsenal, ca. WW-II.

kbg — WW-II German ordnance code assigned to Erwin Backhaus, Remscheid.

kce — WW-II German ordnance code assigned to Schneider & Co., Le Creuot, France.

keb — WW-II German ordnance code assigned to Manufacture d'Armes Nationale de Levallois, Paris.

KENNEDY — Tradename on rifles used by Whitney Arms Co., ca. 1880.

KERNER, E. & CO. — Sporting arms maker in Suhl, Germany from 1935 to 1939.

KESSLER ARMS CO. — Manufacturer of shotguns in Silver Creek, N.Y. 1951-53.

KETTNER, FRANZ — Rifle maker in Suhl, Germany about 1920-25.

KEYSTONE ARMS CO. — Tradename used by E.K. Tryon Co. of Philadelphia, Pa. on revolvers and shotguns.

kfa — WW-II German ordnance code assigned to Staatliches Arsenal, Sarajevo, Yugoslavia.

kfg — WW-II German ordnance code assigned to Staatliches Arsenal, Sarajevo, Yugoslavia.

kfk — WW-II German ordnance code assigned to Dansk Industrie Syndicat, Copenhagen, Denmark.

kgd — WW-II German ordnance code assigned to Junghans, Montagestelle, Exbrucke, Eslass.

K.G.F. — Abbreviation for Koenigliche Gewehrfabrik of Potsdam, Germany.

KIES, FRITZ & CO. — Sporting arms manufacturer in Suhl, Germany from 1922 to 1945.

KILLDEER — Tradename on single shot rifles made by Western Arms Co., ca. 1900.

KIMBALL, J.M. ARMS CO. — Manufacturer of Kimball pistols in Detroit, Mich. about 1955-57.

KIMEL INDUSTRIES — Current importer and distributor in Matthews, N.C.

KIND, ALBRECHT — Berlin, Germany 1922-28.

KING NITRO — Tradename used by J. Stevens Arms Co. on rifles & shotguns.

KING NITRO — Tradename used by Shapleigh Hardware Co. of St. Louis, Mo. on shotguns made by Crescent Fire Arms Co.

KINGSLAND SPECIAL — Tradename used by Geller, Ward, & Hasner of

St. Louis, Mo. on shotguns made by Crescent Fire Arms Co.

KINGSLAND 10 STAR — See Kingsland Special.

KIRK GUN CO. — Tradename used by Farwell, Ozmun, Kirk & Co. of St. Paul, Minn.

KIRRIKALE TUFEK FB. — Government small arms manufacturing plant in Istanbul, Turkey.

KIRTLAND BROTHERS — Rifle and revolver makers in New York City, ca. 1933.

kjj — WW-II German ordnance code assigned to Askania Werke AG, Berlin-Friedenau, Germany.

kkd — WW-II German ordnance code assigned to Wilhelm Stern, Lederwarenfabrik, Posen, Germany.

klb — WW-II German ordnance code assigned to J.F. Eisfeld GmbH, Kieselbach plant.

kle — WW-II German ordnance code assigned to Steyr-Daimler-Puch AG, Warsaw plant, Poland.

KLEINGUENTHER'S — Current importer of sporting arms in Seguin, Tex.

klg — WW-II German ordnance code assigned to Przemot, Prazisions Metallverarbeitung, Litzmannstadt.

kls — WW-II German ordnance code assigned to Steyr-Daimler-Puch AG, Warsaw plant, Poland.

KNAAK, GEORG — Manufacturer of military and sporting arms in Berlin, Germany 1912-45.

KNICKERBOCKER — Tradename on shotguns made by Crescent Fire Arms Co. for H & D Folsom Arms Co.

KNICKERBOCKER — Tradename used by J. Stevens Arms Co. on Model 311 shotguns.

KNOBLE, WM. B. — Designer of Tacoma, Wash. who submitted a pistol to the 1907 U.S. test.

KNOCKABOUT — Tradename used by Montgomery Wards on shotguns made by Crescent Fire Arms Co.

KNOCKABOUT — Tradename used by J. Stevens Arms Co. on Model 311 shotguns.

KNOX-ALL — Tradename on shotguns made by Crescent Fire Arms Co., and later on shotguns by Iver Johnson.

KOBOLD — Tradename on revolvers from Albrecht Kind.

KODIAK — Tradename used by Liberty Arms Organization of Montrose, Calif. on imported revolvers, ca. 1976.

KODIAK MANUFACTURING CO. — North Haven, Conn. manufacturer of long guns. ca. 1965.

KOENIGLICHE GEWEHRFABRIK — Rifle makers in Potsdam, Germany.

KOISHIGAWA — See Kokura Arsenal.

KOKURA ARSENAL — Tokyo, Japan from about 1900 until the end of WW-II. Originally named Koishigawa.

KOLIBRI — Tradename used by Georg Grabner (Austria).

KOLIBRI — Tradename used by Hijos de Francisco Arizaga.

KOMMER, THEODOR — Manufacturer of sporting arms in Zella-Mehlis, Germany 1934-39.

KONIG, H. & A. — Manufacturers of sporting arms in Zella-Mehlis, Germany 1922-39.

KONGSBERG VAPENFABRIK — Government small arms manufacturing plant in Kongsberg, Norway.

KORRIPHILA — Current pistol maker in Ulm/Donau, West Germany.

KORTH — Tradename on revolvers made by Wilhelm Korth Waffenfabrik of Ratzburg, West Germany, a subsidiary of Dynamit Nobel.

KRAUSSER, ALFRED — Sporting arms manufacturer in Zella-Mehlis, Germany 1920-27.

krd — WW-II German ordnance code assigned to Lignose Sprengstoffwerke GmbH, Kriewald.

krg — WW-II German ordnance code assigned to Emil Busch AG, Optische Werke, Budapest, Hungary.

krg — WW-II German ordnance code assigned to Emil Busch AG, Optische Werke, Rathenow, Brandenburg, Germany.

KRICO — Tradename used by Kriegeskorte & Co. of Stuttgart-Hedelfingen, West Germany on sporting arms currently made.

KRIEGESKORTE & CO. — Current manufacturer of sporting arms in Stuttgart-Hedelfingen, West Germany.

KRIEGHOFF, HEINRICH — Manufacturer of military and sporting arms from 1929 until 1945 in Suhl, Germany, and from 1945 until now in Ulm/Donau, West Germany.

krj — WW-II German ordnance code assigned to Messerschmidt, Augsburg.

krl — WW-II German ordnance code assigned to Dynamit AG (formerly Alfred Nobel & Co.) Krummel plant, Koblenz.

KRNKA — Tradename of Oesterreichische Waffenfabrik.

KROYDEN — Tradename used by Savage Arms Corp. on long arms.

kru — WW-II German ordnance code assigned to Lignose Sprengstoffwerke GmbH, Kruppsmuhle plant.

KRUSCHITZ — Tradename on custom arms made in Vienna and imported by Flaig's, ca. 1950.

kry — WW-II German ordnance code assigned to Lignose Sprengstoffwerke GmbH, Kruppsmuhle plant.

ksb — WW-II German ordnance code assigned to Manufacture Nationale d'Armes de Levallois, Levallois, Paris.

ksm — WW-II German ordnance code assigned to Junghans, Braunau plant, Sudeten, Germany.

K.T.G. INDUSTRIAL — Shotgun manufacturer in Hitachi City, Japan.

ktz — WW-II German ordnance code assigned to Deutsche Sprengchemie, Klietz plant, Germany.

kum — WW-II German ordnance code assigned to J.F. Eisfeld, Pulver- u. Pyrotechnische Fabrik GmbH.

kun — WW-II German ordnance code assigned to Lignose Sprengstoffwerke, Kunigunde plant.

kur — WW-II German ordnance code assigned to Steyr-Daimler-Puch AG, Graz, Austria.

kvu — WW-II German ordnance code assigned to Lignose Sprengstoffwerke GmbH, Kruppsmuhle plant.

kwe — WW-II German ordnance code assigned to Gamma Feinmechanik u. Optik, Budapest, Hungary.

kwn — WW-II German ordnance code assigned to S.A. Fiat, Turin, Italy.

kye — WW-II German ordnance code assigned to Intreprinderile Metalurgie, Pumitra Voina Societate, Anonima Romana, Fabrica de Armament, Brasov, Romania.

kyn — WW-II German ordnance code assigned to Astra, Fabrica Romana de Vagone, Motoaene Armament si Munitione, Brasov, Romania.

kyo — WW-II German ordnance code assigned to Intreprinderile Metalurgie, Pumitra Voina Aocietate, Anonima Romana, Fabrica de Armament, Brasov, Romania.

kyp — WW-II German ordnance code assigned to Rumanisch-Deutsche Industrie u. Handels AG, Budapest, Hungary.

kza — Mauser-Werke, Karlsruhe, Germany.

kzn — WW-II German ordnance code assigned to Kienzle, Dammerkirch plant.

L

la — WW-II German ordnance code assigned to Durener Metallwerke, Duren.

LA — Tradename of LA Dist., located in New York City, ca. 1970.

lac — WW-II German ordnance code assigned to Zuchthaus Coswig, Anhalt.

LADIES PET — Tradename used by E.C. Meacham Co. of St. Louis, Mo. on revolvers.

lae — WW-II German ordnance code assigned to Heinrich Zeiss, Gastingen.

LA INDUSTRIA ORBEA — Tradename of Orbea Hermanos.

LAKESIDE — Tradename used by Montgomery, Ward & Co. on shotguns made by Crescent Fire Arms Co.

LA LIRA — Tradename of Garate, Anitua y Cia.

LAMPO — Tradename of C. Torbuzio on pistol.

LA NATIONALE — Tradename on rifles made by Amon of St. Etienne, France.

LANCASTER, CHARLES & CO. — London, England 1867 to 1900, successor to Charles William Lancaster established in 1826. Manufacturers of sporting arms, but best known for big-game hunting pistols. Merged with Stephan Grant & Sons and Lang & Hussey in 1900 to become Joseph Lang & Co., Ltd.

LANDMANN, J.G. — Rifle manufacturer in West Germany, ca. 1968.

LANG & HUSSEY — See Joseph Lang & Co.

LANG, JOSEPH & CO. — Manufacturers of sporting arms in London, England since it was established as Joseph Lang in 1821. In 1874 became Joseph Lang & Son, and in 1896 was changed to Lang & Hussey. In 1900 merged with Charles Lancaster & Co. and Stephan Grant & Sons to form Joseph Lang & Co.

LANGENHAN, EMIL — Manufacturer of sporting arms in Zella-Mehlis, Germany, ca. 1933-38.

LANGENHAN, FRANZ — Manufacturer of sporting arms in Zella-Mehlis, Germany from 1935 to 1939.

LA SALLE — Tradename of Manufrance on shotguns.

LAU, J. H. & CO. — Tradename used by H. & D. Folsom Arms Co.

lax — WW-II German ordnance code assigned to Lennewerk Altena.

ldb — WW-II German ordnance code assigned to Deutsche Pryotechnische Fabriken GmbH, Berlin plant, Malchow, Germany.

ldc — WW-II German ordnance code assigned to Deutsche Pyrotechnische Fabriken GmbH, Cleebronn plant.

ldn — WW-II German ordnance code assigned to Deutsche Pyrotechnische Fabriken GmbH, Neumarkt plant, Oberpfalz.

L.E. — Abbreviation for Larranaga y Elartza.

LEADER — Tradename on revolvers probably made by Hopkins & Allen, ca. 1880.

LEADER GUN CO. — Tradename of Charles William Stores, Inc. of N.Y.C. on shotguns made by Crescent Fire Arms Co.

LEAVELL, CHARLES W. — Sporting arms importer in Sumpter, S.C., ca. 1960.

LEBAU — COURALLY — Current manufacturer of sporting arms in France.

L'ECLAIR — Tradename used by Garate, Anitua y Cia. on revolvers.

LE DRAGON — Tradename of Aguirre y Cia.

LEE ARMS CO. — Manufacturer of "Red Jacket" revolvers in Wilkes-Barre, Pa., ca. 1870.

LEE FIRE ARMS CO. — Bridgeport, Conn. 1879-81, manufacturer of Lee Navy Rifles.

LEE FIREARMS CO. — Milwaukee, Wisc. 1864-65, manufacturers of Lee Carbines.

LEE'S MUNNER SPECIAL — See Lee Special.

LEE SPECIAL — Tradename used by Lee Hardware of Salina, Kansas on shotguns made by Crescent Fire Arms Co.

LEFEVER SONS & CO. — Started in Syracuse, N.Y. as Nichols & Lefever in 1876. In 1879 became D.M. Lefever, in 1889 Lefever Arms Co., and in 1899 Lefever Sons & Co. In 1926 was purchased by Ithaca Gun Co.

LE FRANCAIS — Tradename of Mre. Francais d'Armes et Cycles.

LE FULGOR — Tradename of Charles Clement.

LEGIA — Tradename of Nicolas Pieper.

LEIGH, HENRY — Tradename on shotguns imported from Belgium, ca. 1890.

LE MAJESTIC — Tradename of Mre. d'Armes des Pyrenees.

LEONHARDT — Tradename of H.M. Gering & Co.

LE PAGE — Pistol manufacturer in Liege, Belgium, 1923-30.

LEPPER, MAX — Sporting arms manufacturer in Zella-Mehlis, Germany, ca. 1930.

LE RAPIDE — Tradename of J. Bertrand.

LE SANS PAREIL — Tradename of Mre. d'Armes des Pyrenees.

LE SECOURS — Tradename of Tomas de Urizar y Cia.

LE STEPH — Tradename on pistols made by L. Bergeron of St. Etienne, France.

LE TOUT ACIER — Tradename of Mre. d'Armes des Pyrenees.

LEVER BOLT RIFLE CO. — Manufacturer in New Haven, Conn. 1930-32.

LEWIS, G.E. & SON — Tradename used by Von Lengerke & Detmold of N.Y.C.

lge — WW-II German ordnance code assigned to Kugelfabrik Schulte & Co., Tente, Rheinland, Germany.

L. & H. GUN CO. — Manufactured military style firearms with surplus parts and new or rewelded receivers, 1972-74 San Antonio, Texas. Assets purchased by Springfield Armoury, Geneseo, Ill.

LIBERTY — Tradename on pistols used by Retolaza Hermanos.

LIBERTY — Tradename on revolvers made by Hood Firearms, ca. 1880.

LIBERTY ARMS ORGANIZATION — Current importers of sporting arms in Montrose, Calif.

LIBIA — Tradename used by Beistegui Hermanos.

LICHTMANN, P.R. — Pistol manufacturer in Waltham, Mass. since about 1972.

LIDDLE GUN CO. — See Liddle & Keading.

LIDDLE & KEADING — Established in 1853 as Robert Liddle, name changed to Liddle & Keading in 1872, and to Liddle Gun Co. in 1889. Operated in San Francisco, Calif. until 1894.

LIEGE — Tradename of Mre. Liegeoise d'Armes a Feu.

LIGHTNING — Tradename used on pistols by Echave y Arizmendi.

LIGNOSE — Tradename on Bergmann pistols marketed by Aktien-Ges. Lignose Abteilung of Berlin, Germany, ca. 1930.

LILIPUT — Tradename used by August Menz on pistols.

LION — Tradename used by J.P. Lovell of Boston, Mass. on revolvers made by Johnson, Bye & Co., ca. 1870.

LITHGOW — Royal Australian Small Arms Factory located in New South Wales, Australia making military arms.

LITTLE ALL RIGHT — Tradename used by Wright Arms Co. of Lawrence, Mass. on revolvers, ca. 1875.

LITTLE GIANT — Tradename used on revolvers by Bacon Arms Co., ca. 1880.

LITTLE JOHN — Tradename used by Hood Firearms on revolvers, ca. 1875.

LITTLE JOKER — Tradename on revolvers used by J.M. Malin 1873-75.

LITTLE PAL — Tradename used by Townley Hardware Co. of Kansas City, Mo.

LITTLE PET — Tradename used by J. Stevens Arms Co. on shotguns, and possibly by Hopkins & Allen on revolvers.

LITTLE TOM — Tradename used by Wiener Waffenfabrik on pistols. 71

LJUTIC INDUSTRIES, INC. — Shotgun Manufacturers in current operation in Yakima, Wash.

lkm — WW-II German ordnance code assigned to Munitionsfabriken (formerly Sellier & Bellot), Veitsberg plant, Prague, Czechoslovakia.

LLAMA — Tradename used by Gabilondo y Cia.

lmg — WW-II German ordnance code assigned to Karl Zeiss, Jena.

LOEWE, LUDWIG & CO. — Berlin, Germany 1882 to 1904, manufacturer of contract military arms, primarily known for Mauser style rifles.

LOMBARD — Tradename used by Lombard Co. of Springfield, Mass. on revolvers.

LONG BRANCH — Canadian Arsenals Ltd. (C.A.L.) of Long Branch, Ontario, Canada. Manufacturer of military arms.

LONGINES — Tradename used on pistols by Cooperative Orbea.

LONG RANGE WINNER — See Long Range Wonder.

LONG RANGE WONDER — Tradename used by Sears, Roebuck & Co. on shotguns.

LONG TOM — Tradename used by J. Stevens Arms Co. on shotguns, and by Sears, Roebuck & Co.

LOOKING GLASS — Tradename used by Domingo Acha on hammerless pistols, and by Fernando Acha on hammer model pistols.

LOVELL ARMS CO. — 1840-91 in Boston, Mass. Became J.P. Lovell & Sons about 1870, and was possibly absorbed by Iver Johnson in 1868 but allowed to operate under its existing name.

LOVENA — Tradename used by Janccek of Praha, Czechoslovakia 1930-39.

LOWELL ARMS CO. — Lowell, Mass. 1864-68, made revolvers and carbines.

LOWER, J.P. — Established 1851 in Philadelphia, Pa. In about 1870 moved to Denver, Colo., and became

J.P. Lower's Sons about 1914. Made D.D. Cone revolvers, ca. 1870, and Indian trade guns.

LOYOLA — Tradename on shotguns made in Spain by Jana International of Denver, Colo.

LSA — Tradename on rifles imported by Ithaca Gun Co. from Oy Tikkakoski AB.

ltm — WW-II German ordnance code assigned to Metallwarenfabrik Litzmannstadt.

LUGER — Tradename of Stoeger Industries; used on the P.08 pistol and its copies that are marketed by Stoeger. The name is generally associated with all P.08 pistols (invented by Georg Luger), however, the name is copyrighted by Stoeger.

LUNEBURG, AUGUST — Sporting arms manufacturer in Kiel, Germany, ca. 1930.

LUR — Tradename used by Echave y Arizmendi y Cia.

lwg — WW-II German ordnance code assigned to Optische Werke Osterrode GmbH, Freiheit near Osterrode.

lww — WW-II German ordnance code assigned to Huet & Cie., Paris, France.

lwx — WW-II German ordnance code assigned to O.P.L. Optique et Precision de Levallois, Levallois, Paris.

lwy — WW-II German ordnance code assigned to Societe Optique et Mechanique de Haute Precision, Paris.

lyf — WW-II German ordnance code assigned to Metallurgia Werke AG, Radomsko, Poland.

LYMAN GUN SIGHT CORP. — Distributors of blackpowder arms private-labeled by Navy Arms.

LYNX — Tradename on revolvers made in South Africa and distributed by Nitro Wholesalers of Johannesburg.

lza — WW-II German ordnance code assigned to Mauser-Werke AG, Karlsruhe plant, Germany.

M

ma — WW-II German ordnance code assigned to Metallwerke Lange AG, Aue, Saxony, Germany.

M.A.B. — Abbreviation for Mre. D'Armes Automatiques Bayonne.

M.A.C. — Abbreviation for Military Armament Corp. on submachine guns and silencers.

MALTBY-CURTIS — Distributors of revolvers made by Norwich Falls Pistol Co. 1875-81, located in New York City.

MALTBY-HENLEY & CO. — Distributors of revolvers made by Columbia Armory 1878-89, located in New York City.

MAMBA — Tradename on pistols developed by Relay Products (Pty) Ltd. of Johannesburg, South Africa, and also made in the U.S. by Navy Arms.

MANDALL SHOOTING SUPPLIES, INC. — Current importers established 1953 in Brooklyn, N.Y., in 1975 moved to Scottsdale, Ariz.

MANHATTAN FIREARMS CO. — Manufacturer of handguns in New York City and Newark, N.J. starting in 1849. About 1870 became American Standard Tool Co.

MANHATTAN ARMS CO. — Tradename used by Schoverling, Daly & Gales of N.Y.C., ca. 1900.

MANNLICHER-SCHOENAUER— Tradename used on rifles by Steyr Daimler Puch of Steyr, Austria.

MANNLICHER WAFFENFABRIK — Arms manufacturer in Steyr, Austria, ca. 1905.

MAN STOPPER — Tradename on pistols from Charles Lancaster & Co., ca. 1890.

MANTON, J. & CO. — Tradename on Belgian shotguns, ca. 1900, not to be confused with Joseph Manton & Son Co. of London, England.

MANTON, JOSEPH & SON CO. — Sporting arms makers in London, England from 1835. Before then was Joseph Manton, established 1795. Maintained a Calcutta, India branch 1840-77.

MANUFACTURE D'ARMERO — ESPECIALISTS REUNIDES — Handgun manufacturer in Eibar, Spain, 1924-27.

MANUFACTURA DE ARMAS DE FUEGO — Guernica, Spain about 1922. Reputed to be the name of Alkartasuna (q.v.) after that company ceased operations.

MANUFRANCE — Tradename of Mre. Francais d'Armes et Cycles.

MANURHIN — Tradename of Manufacture de Machines du Haut-Rhin, France.

MARBLE ARMS & MFG. CO. — Gladstone, Mich. from 1898. In 1908 they made "Game Getter" rifles and shotguns.

MARHOLT, RICHARD — Manufacturer of sporting arms in Innsbruck, Austria, ca. 1954.

MARINA — Tradename of Gregorio Bolumburu.

MARIXA — Manufacturer of sporting arms in Eibar, Spain.

MARKE — Tradename of Hijos de Jorge Bascaran.

MARKSMAN — Tradename used on rifles made by H. Pieper of Liege, Belgium, ca. 1900.

MARKWELL ARMS CO. — Current manufacturer and importer of blackpowder arms in Chicago, Ill.

MARK X — Tradename on rifles imported by Interarms on arms made by Zavodi Crvena Zastava of Belgrade, Yugoslavia.

MARLIN FIREARMS CO. — New Haven, Conn. from 1870 when it was established as J.M. Marlin. In 1881 became Marlin Firearms Co., in 1915 became Marlin-Rockwell Corp., and in 1926 Marlin Firearms Co. again. Made sporting and military arms including Ballard rifles (1875) and L.C. Smith shotguns (1948).

MARQUIS OF LORNE — Tradename on revolvers made by Hood Firearms Co., ca. 1880.

MARS — Tradename on .25 acp pistols used by Posumavska Zbrojovka Kdyne, of Kdyne, Czechoslovakia.

MARS — Model of Gabbett-Fairfax made by Webley and Scott of Birmingham, England, ca. 1900.

MARS — Tradename on .32 acp pistols used by Kohout & Spol (Czechoslovakia).

MARS EQUIPMENT — Importers of sporting arms in Chicago, Ill., ca. 1970.

MARSHWOOD — Tradename used by Charles Williams Stores of New York City.

MARSHWOOD — Tradename used by J. Stevens Arms Co. on shotguns.

MARSON, SAMUEL & CO. — Manufacturer of military and sporting arms in Birmingham, England established in 1840.

MARTE — Tradename of Erquiaga, Muguruza y Cia.

MARTIAN — Tradename of Martin A. Bascaran used on pistols.

MARTIGNY — Tradename of Hijos de Jorge Bascaran.

M.A.S. — Abbreviation for Mre. d'Armes de Saint Etienne.

MASSACHUSETTS ARMS — Tradename used by J. Stevens Arms Co. on shotguns.

MASSACHUSETTS ARMS CO. — Tradename used by Blish, Mize, & Silliman Hardware of Atchison, Kansas.

M.A.T. — Abbreviation for Mre. d'Armes de Tuile.

MATADOR — Tradename on shotguns made in Spain and imported by Firearms International.

MATHIEW ARMS CO. — Manufacturer of rifles in Oakland, Calif. from about 1950 to about 1960.

MAUSER-BAUER — Importers of Mauser sporting arms in Frazer, Mich. about 1971-74.

MAUSER RIFLE — Term applied to rifles based on the Mauser bolt-action system, but not necessarily denoting origin.

MAUSER WERKE AG. — Established as Gebr. Mauser et Cie. 1864, name changed to Mauser Werke Ag. in 1890. Also called Waffenfabrik Mauser, it's located in Oberndorf, Germany. Manufacturers of both sporting and military weapons.

MAVERICK DERRINGER — Tradename used by Intercontinental Arms, importers in Los Angeles, Calif., ca. 1970.

MAXIM — Tradename used by Hy Hunter Corp. on pistols imported from Italy, possibly Rigarmi, ca. 1960.

MAYOR ARQUEBUSER — Tradename on pistols used by Francois Mayor on Rochat patent pistols.

MAYOR, FRANCOIS II — Manufacturer of Rochat patent pistols in Lausanne, Switzerland. In business from 1925 to 1959.

M & B — Abbreviation for Merwin & Bray (see Merwin, Hulbert & Co.).

MCA — Tradename used by Steyr Daimler Puch on rifles made in Steyr, Austria.

MCK — Tradename and abbreviation for McKeown's Guns on Italian shotguns.

MCKEOWN'S GUNS — Importer of Italian shotguns in Pekin, Ill. since 1970.

mdr — WW-II German ordnance code assigned to Vereinigte Leichtmetallwerke, Bonn, Germany.

MECURY — Tradename on pistols made by Robar et Cie.

MEFFERT, M. — Manufacturer of shotguns in Berlin, Germany, ca. 1910.

MELIOR — Tradename of Robar et Cie., used on pistols.

MENTA — Tradename of August Menz.

MERCURY — Tradename on shotguns imported by Tradewinds of Tacoma, Wash.

MERIDEN FIREARMS CO. — Meriden, Conn. 1907-09, makers of revolvers and rifles, subsidiary of Sears, Roebuck & Co.

MERRILL CO. — Current manufacturers of handguns in Rockwell City, Iowa.

MERWIN & BRAY — See Merwin, Hulbert & Co.

MERWIN, HULBERT & CO. — Distributors and manufacturers agents in New York City starting about 1853 as Merwin & Bray. Between 1864 and 1868 the name changed to Merwin & Simpkins, and to Merwin, Taylor & Simpkins, and finally to Merwin, Hulbert & Co. In 1892 the company became Hulbert Bros., and then failed in 1896.

METEOR — Tradename used by J. Stevens Arms Co. on rifles.

METEOR RIFLES — Tradename used by Shapleigh Hardware Co. of St. Louis, Mo.

METROPOLITAN — Tradename used by Siegel Cooper Co. of N.Y.C. on shotguns made by Crescent Fire Arms Co.

METROPOLITAN POLICE — Tradename on revolvers made by Norwich Falls Pistol Co., ca. 1885.

MERWIN & BRAY — See Merwin, Hulbert & Co.

MERWIN & SIMPKINS — See Merwin, Hulbert & Co.

MERWIN-TAYLOR & SIMPKINS — See Merwin, Hulbert & Co.

M.F. — Abbreviation for Mre. Francaise d'Armes et Cycles.

M.H. & CO. — Abbreviation for Merwin, Hulbert & Co.

mhk — WW-II German ordnance code assigned to Metallwerke Schwarzwald AG, Villingen.

mhv — WW-II German ordnance code assigned to Finow Kipfer- u. Messingwerke AG, Finow.

MIIDA — Tradename on shotguns imported by Marubeni America Corp. from Japan.

MIKROS — Tradename of Mre. d'Armes des Pyrenees on pistols made 1934-39, and from 1958 to date.

MILITAR — Tradename used by Hy Hunter of Burbank, Calif. on imported pistols, ca. 1960.

MINERVE — Tradename on pistols marketed by Fab. d'Armes de Grande Precision.

MINIMA — Tradename of M. Boyer.

MINNEAPOLIS FIREARMS CO. — Manufacturers of palm pistols in Minneapolis, Minn., ca. 1891.

MINNESOTA ARMS CO. — Tradename used by Farwell, Ozmun & Kirk of St. Paul, Minn.

MIROKU, B.C. — Current manufacturer of sporting arms in Japan.

MISSISSIPPI VALLEY ARMS CO. — Tradename used by Shapleigh Hardware of St. Louis on shotguns made by Crescent Fire Arms Co.

mjr — WW-II German ordnance code assigned to Union Gesellschaft fur Met. Ind., Sils van de Loo & Co., Thorn plant.

MKE — Tradename of Kirikkale Tufek Fb. of Kirikkale, Turkey, used on Walther PP copies.

mkf — WW-II German ordnance code assigned to Trierer Walzwerk, Wuppertal-Langerfeld.

M.L. — Abbreviation for Mre. Liegeoise d'Armes a. Feu of Liege, Belgium.

mnf — WW-II German ordnance code assigned to VDM Heddernheim, Frankfurt on the Main, Germany.

mng — WW-II German ordnance code assigned to VDM Heddernheim, Frankfurt on the Main, Germany.

moc — WW-II German ordnance code assigned to Johan Springer's Erben, Gewehrfabrikanten, Vienna, Austria.

mog — WW-II German ordnance code assigned to Deutsche Sprengchemie, Moschweig plant.

MOHAWK — Tradename used by Blish, Mize & Steelman of Atchison, Kansas on shotguns made by Crescent Fire Arms Co.

MOHAWK ARMS CO. — Tradename used by Remington Arms Co.

MONARCH — Tradename used by Hopkins & Allen on revolvers labeled "#1" to "#4", ca. 1880.

MONARCH — Tradename used by Osgood Gun Works of Norwich, Conn. on revolvers, ca. 1882.

MONDIAL — Tradename on pistols, used by Gaspar Arizaga.

MONITOR — Tradename used by Paxton, Gallagher & Co. of Omaha, Nebr.

MONITOR — Tradename used by J. Stevens Arms Co. on shotguns.

MONOBLOCK — Tradename on pistols made by J. Jacquemart of Herstal, Belgium.

MONTE CARLO — Tradename used by J.L. Galef & Son, Inc. of N.Y.C.

moo — WW-II German ordnance code assigned to Klockner-Werke AG, Dusseldorf plant, Germany.

MOORE PATENT FIREARMS CO. — Brooklyn, N.Y. 1863-83, manufacturer of handguns.

MORRONE — Tradename of Rhode Island Arms Co.

MOSSBERG, O.F. & SONS — Sporting arms manufacturer in New Haven, Conn. since 1919. Before that was Oscar F. Mossberg from 1892.

MOUNTAIN ARMS, INC. — Manufacturer of .22 rifles in Ozark, Mo., ca. 1976.

MOUNTAIN EAGLE — Tradename used by Hopkins & Allen on revolvers, ca. 1880.

moz — WW-II German ordnance code assigned to Eisenwerk Gesellschaft Maximilianhutte, Maxhutte-Haidhof.

mpp — WW-II German ordnance code assigned to Metallwerk K. Leibfried, Boblingen, Sindelfingen plant.

mpr — WW-II German ordnance code assigned to S.A. Hispano Suiza, Geneva, Switzerland.

mpv — WW-II German ordnance code assigned to Schmolz u. Bickenbach, Neuss plant, Dusseldorf, Germany.

mpy — WW-II German ordnance code assigned to Klockner-Werke AG, Georgsmarienhutte Osnabruck.

mrb — WW-II German ordnance code assigned to Skodawerke, Prague Plant, Smichow, Czechoslovakia.

mrd — WW-II German ordnance code assigned to Huttenwerke Siegerland, Wissen.

MRE. D'ARMES DES PYRENEES — Manufacturers of sporting arms in Hendaye, France since 1930.

MRE. FRANCAISE D'ARMES ET CYCLES — Sporting arms manufacturer in St. Etienne, France since 1920.

mrf — WW-II German ordnance code assigned to Fr. Krupp, Berthawerk AG, Breslau.

M.S. — Abbreviation for Modesto Santos, used on "Action" pistols.

MT. VERNON ARMS — Tradename used on shotguns imported from Belgium, ca. 1900.

MULHOUSE — Tradename of Manufacture de Machines du Haut-Rhin, France.

MUSKETEER — Tradename on rifles with F.N. actions made by Firearms International, ca. 1968.

M.W. & CO. — Abbreviation of Montgomery, Ward & Co.

mws — WW-II German ordnance code assigned to Munitionswerke Schonebeck.

MY COMPANION — Tradename on revolvers made by Hopkins & Allen, ca. 1870.

MY FRIEND — Tradename used by James Reid on "Knuckleduster" revolvers.

myx — WW-II German ordnance code assigned to Rheinmetall-Borsig AG, Sommerda plant.

N

na — WW-II German ordnance code assigned to Westfalische Kupfer- u. Messingwerke AG, Ludenscheid, Westphalia, Germany.

NAACO — Abbreviation for North American Arms Co. in Quebec, Canada on M1911 pistols, ca. 1918.

NAGOYA ARSENAL — Japanese military weapons plant, ca. WW-II.

NAPOLEON — Tradename used on revolvers by Thomas Ryan, Jr. Pistol Mfg. Co. 1870-76.

NARODNI PODNIK — Czechoslovakian rifle maker post- WW-II.

nas — WW-II German ordnance code assigned to Uhrenfabrik Junghans, Schramberg, Black Forest, Germany.

NATIONAL — Tradename used by Norwich Falls Pistol Co. on revolvers, ca. 1880.

NATIONAL ARMS CO. — Tradename on shotguns from Crescent Fire Arms Co.

NATIONAL FIREARMS CO. — Tradename used by Hopkins & Allen on rifles, ca. 1900.

NATIONAL ORDNANCE, INC. — 1965-74 manufactured and assembled from parts military style firearms. South El Monte, Calif.

NAT ORD — Abbreviation for National Ordnance, Inc.

NATIONAL POSTAL METER — Manufacturer of M-1 Carbines during WW-II in Rochester, N.Y. Its name at the start of production was Rochester Defense Corp., and at the end of production the name changed to Commercial Controls Corp.

nb — WW-II German ordnance code assigned to Waffenfabrik Kongsberg, Norway.

nbe — WW-II German ordnance code assigned to Hasag, Eisen- u. Metallwerke GmbH, Tachenstocha plant.

nbh — WW-II German ordnance code assigned to Walther Steiner, Eisenkonstruktionen Suhl, Germany.

nbr — WW-II German ordnance code assigned to Metallwarenfabrik Hubert Prunte, Neheim-Husten, Germany.

ncr — WW-II German ordnance code assigned to Krupp-Germaniawerft, Kiel-Gaarden, Germany.

ndr — WW-II German ordnance code assigned to Krupp Essen.

nea — WW-II German ordnance code assigned to Walther Steiner, Eisenkonstruktionen, Suhl, Germany.

nec — WW-II German ordnance code assigned to Waffenwerke Brunn AG, V Gurein plant, Prague, Czechoslovakia.

ned — WW-II German ordnance code assigned to Krupp, Essen.

NEDERLANDISCHE WAPENEN MUNITIEFABRIK — See NWM.

NERO — Tradename used by E. Tryon Co. on revolvers made by J. Rupertus Arms Co., ca. 1880. The same name is also used by C.L. Riker on revolvers of the same general type made by Hopkins & Allen, ca. 1880.

NEUHAUSEN PISTOL — Term applied to the P.210 pistol made by S.I.G. at Neuhausen, Switzerland.

NEVER MISS — Tradename used by Hopkins & Allen and J.M. Marlin on revolvers, ca. 1875.

NEW CHIEFTAIN — Tradename used by J. Stevens Arms Co. on shotguns.

NEW ENGLAND ARMS CO. — Tradename used by Charles J. Godfrey of N.Y.C., and by Rohde, Spencer Co. of Chicago, Ill., ca. 1900.

NEW HAVEN — Tradename on long guns used by O.F. Mossberg & Sons.

NEW LIBERTY — Tradename used by Sears, Roebuck & Co.

NEW NAMBU — Tradename on copies of Colt M1911A1 pistols made in Japan by Shin Chau Kogyo of Tokyo.

NEWPORT — Tradename used by Hibbard, Spencer, Bartlett Co. of Chicago, Ill.

NEWPORT — Tradename used by J. Stevens Arms Co. on shotguns.

NEW RIVAL — Tradename used by Van Camp Hdw. & Iron Co. of Indianapolis, Ind. on shotguns made by Crescent Fire Arms. Co.

NEWTON ARMS CO. — Manufacturer of rifles in Buffalo, N.Y. starting in 1914. In 1918 failed, and was reorganized in 1919 as Newton Rifle Corp., which continued until 1930.

NEWTON RIFLE CORP. — See Newton Arms Co.

NEW WORCESTER — Tradename on shotguns made by Torkelson Arms Co., ca. 1905.

NEW YORK ARMS CO. — Tradename used by Garnet Carter Co. of Chattanooga, Tenn. on shotguns made by Crescent Fire Arms Co.

NEW YORK PISTOL CO. — Revolver makers in New York City, ca. 1870.

nfx — WW-II German ordnance code assigned to Rheinisch-Westfalische Munitionsfabriken GmbH, plants in Warsaw and Prague, Czechoslovakia.

nhr — WW-II German ordnance code assigned to Rheinmetall-Borsig AG, Sommerda plant, Germany.

NIKKO ARMS CO. LTD. — Current manufacturer of sporting arms in Tochigi City, Japan.

925 — WW-II German ordnance code assigned to Mauser-Werke, Oberndorf on the Neckar, Germany.

945 — WW-II German ordnance code assigned to Waffenfabrik Brunn AG, Brno, Czechoslovakia.

1924 MODEL — Marking on S & W revolver copy made in Eibar, Spain by Fabrica de Armas Garantazadas.

NITRO BIRD — Tradename on shotguns used by Richards & Conover Hardware Co. of Kansas City, Mo.

NITRO HUNTER — Tradename on shotguns used by Belknap Hardware Co. of Louisville, Ky.

NITRO PROOF — Tradename used by J. Stevens Arms Co. on shotguns.

NITRO SPECIAL — Tradename used by J. Stevens Arms Co. on shotguns.

NIVA — Tradename of Kohout & Spol on pistols made in Czechoslovakia.

nmn — WW-II German ordnance code assigned to Konigs- u. Bismarckhutte AG, Walzwerk Bismarckhutte-OS.

NOBLE MFG. CO., INC. — Rifle and shotgun maker in Haydenville, Mass. 1950-71.

NONPARIEL — Tradename of revolvers made by Norwich Falls Pistol Co., ca. 1880.

NORRAHAMMER — Tradename on HVA rifles imported by Tradewinds.

NORTH AMERICAN ARMS CO. — Quebec, Canada, ca. 1918, manufacturer of M1911 pistols.

NORTHWESTERNER — Tradename used by J. Stevens Arms Co. on rifles and shotguns.

NORWICH ARMS CO. — Tradename on revolvers probably used by Norwich Falls Pistol Co., ca. 1880.

NORWICH ARMS CO. — Tradename used on shotguns by Crescent Fire Arms Co.

NOT-NAC MFG. CO. — Tradename used by Belknap Hdw. Co. of Louisville, Ky. on shotguns made by Crescent Fire Arms Co.

nrh — WW-II German ordnance code assigned to Rheinmetall-Borsig, Sommerda, Germany.

NUMRICH ARMS CO. — Current manufacturers of sporting and black-powder arms, machine guns, and parts. Present owners of Auto Ordnance (Thompson submachine guns) and Hopkins & Allen. Located in West Hurley, N.Y.

NWM — Abbreviation for Nederlandische Wapenen Munitiefabrik in S'Hertogenbosch, Holland, manufacturer of military and sporting arms.

nxr — WW-II German ordnance code assigned to Anschutz & Co., Kiel-Neumuhlen, Germany.

nyv — WW-II German ordnance code assigned to Rheinmetall-Borsig AG, Unterlass plant.

nyw — WW-II German ordnance code assigned to Gustloff-Werke, Otto Eberhard, Meinigen plant.

O

oa — WW-II German ordnance code assigned to Eduard Huck, Metallwalzwerk, Ludenscheid.

OAK LEAF — Tradename of J. Stevens Arms Co. on shotguns.

oao — WW-II German ordnance code assigned to Anschutz, Kiel-Neumuhlen.

obn — WW-II German ordnance code assigned to Hagenuk, Reichenbach plant.

OCCIDENTAL — Tradename on shotguns made in Belgium and imported about 1890.

ocw — WW-II German ordnance code assigned to Heinrich List, Berlin-Steglitz, Germany.

odg — WW-II German ordnance code assigned to Deutsche Sprengchemie, Oderberg plant, Germany.

oes — WW-II German ordnance code assigned to Karl Diehl, Peterswaldau.

O.H. — Abbreviation for Orbea Hermanos on revolvers.

OJANGURAN Y VIDOSA — Handgun manufacturers in Eibar, Spain 1922-38.

OKZET — Tradename of August Menz.

OLD TIMER — Tradename used by J. Stevens Arms Co. on shotguns.

OLIN KODENSHA CO. LTD. — Manufacturer of shotguns in Tokyo, Japan, in current production.

ols — WW-II German ordnance code assigned to Union Ges. fur Metallindustrie, Sils van de Loo, Auschwitz.

OLYMPIC — Tradename used by J. Stevens Arms Co. on Model 311, 315 and 94 shotguns sold by Morley & Murphey Hdw. Co. of Green Bay, Wisc.

O.M.C. — Abbreviation for Ordnance Mfg. Corp., division of T.D.E. Marketing in south El Monte, Calif.

OMEGA — Tradename of rifles made by Hi-Shear Corp.

OMEGA — Tradename of Industria Orbea Armera on pistols.

OMEGA — Tradename used by Gerstenberger & Eberwein on revolvers with drop-out cylinders.

OMEGA — Tradename used by Herman Weihrauch Sportwaffenfabrik on revolvers with swing-out cylinders.

OMNIPOL — Czechoslovakian arms export organisation in Prague.

122 — WW-II German ordnance code assigned to Hugo Schmeisser.

ORBEA — Orbea Hermanos, manufacturer of handguns in Eibar, Spain 1916-22.

OREA — Tradename on Heeren rifles made by Orechowsky of Graz, Austria, ca. 1930.

OSGOOD GUN WORKS — Manufacturer of revolvers in Norwich, Conn., ca. 1882.

O.V. — Abbreviation for Ojanguran y Vidosa.

O.W.A. — Abbreviation for Oesterreichische Werke gws. Anstalt on pistols, ca. 1925 (Austria).

OXFORD ARMS CO. — Tradename used by J. Stevens Arms Co. on shotguns.

OXFORD ARMS CO. — Tradename used by Belknap Hardware of Louisville, Ky. on shotguns made by Crescent Fire Arms Co.

oxo — WW-II German ordnance code assigned to Teuto-Metallwerke GmbH, Osnabruck.

OYEZ ARMS CO. — Pistol makers in Liege, Belgium.

OY TIKKAKOSKI AB — Rifle manufacturers in Tikkakoski, Finland from about 1964, imported under the tradenames "Tikka" and "Ithaca-LSA."

oyj — WW-II German ordnance code assigned to Atelier de Construction de Tarbes, France.

P

p — WW-II German ordnance code assigned to Polte Armaturen- u. Maschinenfabrik AG, Magdeburg, Saxony, Germany.

p — WW-II German ordnance code assigned to Ruhrstahl, Brackwede, Germany.

pad — WW-II German ordnance code assigned to T. Bergmann & Co., Bernau plant, Berlin, Germany.

P.A.F. — Abbreviation for Pretoria Arms Factory manufacturer of the "Junior" pocket pistol, ca. 1955; assets purchased by B.R.F. about 1956.

PAGE-LEWIS ARMS CO. — Chicopee Fall, Mass. about 1920. Manufactured rifles and was purchased by J. Stevens Arms Co. in 1926.

PAGOMA — Tradename used by Paxton & Gallagher Co. of Omaha, Nebr., ca. 1910.

PALMETTO — Tradename used by J. Stevens Arms Co. on shotguns.

PANTAX — Tradename of E. Woerther of Buenos Aires, Argentina on pistols.

PANZER — Tradename used on imported pistols by Hy Hunter of Burbank, Calif., ca. 1960.

PARAGON — Tradename used on revolvers probably by Hopkins & Allen, ca. 1880.

PARAGON — Tradename used by J. Stevens Arms Co. on shotguns.

PARAMOUNT — Tradename of Retolaza Hermanos, of Eibar, Spain, used on pistols.

PARKER-BALLARD — Importers of Marixa shotguns in Wilmington, Delaware.

PARKER BROS. — Meriden, Mass. 1868 until being taken over by Remington Arms Co. in 1934. Shotgun makers.

PARKER BROS. — Tradename used in the mid-1970's by Jana International Co. on shotguns imported from Italy.

PARKER-HALE — Current manufacturers of rifles and blackpowder arms in Birmingham, England.

PARKER SAFETY HAMMERLESS — Tradename used by Columbia Armory, Columbia, Tenn., ca. 1890 on revolvers.

PARKHURST, WILLIAM — Arms maker in Bristol, England, ca. 1920.

PAROLE — Tradename used by Hopkins & Allen on revolvers, ca. 1880.

PATHFINDER — Tradename used by Hopkins & Allen on revolvers, ca. 1870.

PATRIOT — Tradename used on revolvers by Norwich Falls Pistol Co., ca. 1880.

pcd — WW-II German ordnance code assigned to T. Bergmann & Co., Gernau plant, Berlin, Germany.

PEDERSEN CUSTOM GUNS — Division of O.F. Mossberg & Sons.

PEERLESS — Tradename used on shotguns by Crescent Fire Arms Co. on guns for H & D Folsom Co.

PEERLESS — Tradename used by J. Stevens Arms Co. on rifles.

PELICAN — Tradename used by Ogilvie Hardware Co. of Shreveport, La.

PENETRATOR — Tradename used on revolvers by Norwich Falls Pistol Co., ca. 1880.

PERAZZI — (Manifattura Armi Perazzi) Current manufacturer of shotguns in Brescia, Italy, imported by Ithaca.

PERFECT — Tradename on revolvers made by Foehl & Weeks, ca. 1890.

PERFECT — Tradename used on pistols by Mre. d'Armes des Pyrenees.

PERFECTION — Tradename used by H. & G. Lipscomb & Co. of Nashville, Tenn. on shotguns by Crescent Firearms Co.

PERFECTION AUTOMATIC REVOLVER — Tradename used by Forehand Arms Co. on revolvers, ca. 1890.

PERLA — Tradename on pistols of Czechoslovakian origin.

PET-PAT — Tradename used by Hopkins & Allen on revolvers, ca. 1870.

P & G — Abbreviation for Paxton & Gallagher Co. of Omaha, Nebr.

PHOENIX — Tradename used on rifles by Whitney Arms Co., ca. 1880.

PHOENIX — Tradename used by Tomas de Urizar y Cia. on pistols (Spain).

PHOENIX ARMS CO. — Lowell, Mass., ca. 1920, makers of pocket pistols.

PIC — Abbreviation and tradename for Precise Imports Corp. in Suffern, N.Y.

PIEDMONT — Tradename used by Piedmont Hardware of Danville, Pa. on shotguns made by Crescent Fire Arms Co.

PIEPER ARMS CO. — See Henri Pieper.

PIEPER, HENRI — Manufacturer of sporting arms in Liege, Belgium from 1884 to 1907 when company became Ancions Etablissments Pieper. (Nicolas Pieper).

PINAFORE — Tradename on revolvers from Norwich Falls Pistol Co., ca. 1880.

PINKERTON — Tradename used by Gaspar Arizaga on pistols.

PIONEER — Tradename used by J. Stevens Arms Co. on rifles.

PIONEER ARMS CO. — Tradename used by Kruse Hardware Co. of Cincinnati, Ohio on shotguns made by Crescent Fire Arms Co.

PIST.AUT. MOD. 1913 — Marking on Campo Giro 9mm pistol Model 1913 made by Esperanza y Unceta.

PIST. AUT. MOD. 1913-16 — Marking on Campo Giro Model 1913/16 9mm pistol made by Esperanza y Unceta.

PITTSFIELD — Tradename used by Hibbard, Spencer & Bartlett Co. of Chicago, Ill.

pjj — WW-II German ordnance code assigned to Haerens Ammunitionsarsenalet, Copenhagen, Denmark.

PJK, INC. — Manufacturer of the J & R M-68 carbine in Bradbury, Calif.

PLAINFIELD MACHINE CO. — Current manufacturers of M-1 carbines and their variations in Dunellen, N.J.

PLAINFIELD ORDNANCE CO. —

Current manufacturers of pistols in Middlesex, N.J.

PLINKER — Tradename on Rohm revolvers which are also marked "Thalco."

PLUS ULTRA — Tradename used on long-grip pistols by Gabilondo y Cia.

PMC — Abbreviation for Plainfield Machine Corp. on carbines.

POINTER — Tradename used by Miroku on automatic shotguns.

POPULAIRE — Tradename on single-shot bolt action pistols made by Mre. Francaise d'Armes et Cycles.

POWELL & CLEMENT — Established in 1839 as Palemon Powell in Cincinnati, Ohio. In 1856 became Powell & Brown, and in 1858 P. Powell; 1870 Powell & Son, and finally Powell & Clement about 1891. Manufacturer of rifles and shotguns.

POWERMAG — Tradename on revolvers imported by Herter's, Inc.

POWERMASTER — Tradename on single-shot pistols made by Wamo Mfg. Co.

PRAGA — Tradename used by Zbrojovka Praga on pistols.

PRAIRIE KING — Tradename on revolvers from Norwich Falls Pistol Co., ca. 1880.

PRECISE — Tradename of PIC on handguns.

PREMIER — Importers of shotguns in Brooklyn, N.Y. since 1955.

PREMIER — Tradename on rifles used by J. Stevens Arms Co.

PREMIER — Tradename used by Thomas E. Ryan on revolvers, ca. 1870.

PREMIER — Tradename of Tomas de Urizar y Cia. on pistols (Spain).

PREMIER — Tradename used by Montgomery, Ward & Co.

PREMIER TRAIL BLAZER — Tradename used on rifles by J. Stevens Arms Co.

PRICE, J.W. — Tradename used by J. Stevens Arms Co. on shotguns.

PRIDE OF BRAZIL — Tradename on shotguns imported by Firearms Import & Export and made by I.N.A. in Brazil.

PRIDE OF SPAIN — Tradename used on shotguns imported by Sloan's in New York City.

PROGRESS — Tradename used by Charles J. Godfrey of New York City.

PROTECTOR — Tradename used by Echave y Arizmendi on pistols.

PROTECTOR — Tradename used by Norwich Falls Pistol Co. on revolvers, ca. 1880.

PROTECTOR — Tradename used by Santigo Salaberrin.

PS — Abbreviation on Italian military arms meaning Publica Sicurezza (Police).

PUCCINELLI COMPANY — Manufacturer and importer since 1964. Established in Brescia, Italy, now also located in San Anselmo, Calif. Developer of the IAB shotgun.

PURDEY, JAMES & SONS — Sporting arms makers in London, England since 1816.

pvf — WW-II German ordnance code assigned to Optische Werke O. Reichert, Vienna, Austria.

P.Z.K. — Abbreviation for Posumavska Zbrojovka.

Q

qa — WW-II German ordnance code assigned to William Prym, Stolberg, Rheinland, Germany.

qrb — WW-II German ordnance code assigned to Pyrotechnische Fabrik, Bologna, Italy.

QUACKENBUSH, H.M. — Manufacturer of rifles and air guns in Herkimer, N.Y., ca. 1880.

QUAIL — Tradename used by Crescent Fire Arms Co. on shotguns.

QUAILS FARGO — Tradename used by Dakin Gun Co., and after 1965 by Simmons Specialties, Inc. of Olathe, Kansas.

QUALITY HARDWARE AND MACHINE CO. — Manufacturer of M-1 carbines during WW-II in Chicago, Ill.

QUEEN CITY — Tradename of Elmira Arms Co. on shotguns made by Crescent Fire Arms Co.

qve — WW-II German ordnance code assigned to Karl Walther, Zella-Mehlis, Thuringia, Germany.

R

r — WW-II German ordnance code assigned to Westfalische-Anhaltische Sprengstoff AG, Reinsdorf plant.

ra — WW-II German ordnance code assigned to Deutsche Messingwerke, C. Eveking AG, Berlin-Niederschonweide, Germany.

RA — Abbreviation on Italian military arms meaning Regia Aeronautica (Air Force).

R.A. — Abbreviation and tradename of Republic Arms, current handgun makers in Johannesburg, South Africa.

RADIUM — Tradename on pistols possibly made by Gabilondo y Urresti.

RADOM — Term used to describe the VIS Model 35 pistol made by Fabryka Broni w Radomiu in Poland.

RALOCK — Tradename used by B.S.A. on semi-auto rifles.

RANGER — Tradename used on revolvers by Hopkins & Allen, ca. 1880.

RANGER — Tradename used by Firearms International on pistols made by Mre. d'Armes des Pyrenees.

RANGER — Tradename on rifles and shotguns from J. Stevens Arms Co.

RANGER — Tradename used by Sears, Roebuck & Co. on various arms, ca. 1925.

RANGER ARMS — Rifle maker in Gainesville, Tex. in the early 1970's, best known for the "Texas Magnum" rifles.

RE — Abbreviation on Italian military arms meaning Regia Esercito (Royal Army).

RECK SPORTWAFFENFABRIK — Postwar manufacturer of handguns in Lauf/Pegnitz, West Germany. Imported into the U.S. until 1968 under many brand names.

RED CHIEFTAIN — Tradename used by Supplee, Biddle Hdw. Co. of Philadelphia, Pa.

RED JACKET — Tradename on revolvers made by Lee Arms, ca. 1870.

REFORM — Tradename used by August Schueler of Suhl, Germany on 4-barrel pistols, ca. 1904.

REGENT — Tradename used on revolvers by Karl Burgsmuller in West Germany.

REGENT — Tradename on revolvers used by Firearms International in the U.S.

REGENT — Tradename used on pistols by Gregorio Bolumburu.

REGINA — Tradename of Gregorio Bolumburu on pistols.

REGNUM — Tradename used by August Menz of Suhl, Germany on 4-barrel pistols.

REIMS PATENT — Tradename of Azanza y Arrizabalaga on pistols.

REINA — Tradename on rifles made by Manufrance.

REINA — Tradename of Mre. d'Armes des Pyrenees on pistols.

RELIABLE — Tradename on revolvers used by Hopkins & Allen, ca. 1880.

RELIANCE — Tradename used by Meunier Gun Co. of Milwaukee, Wisc., ca. 1880.

REMINGTON ARMS CO. — Established in 1816 by Eliphalet Remington in Herkimer County, N.Y. In 1831 moved to Ilion, N.Y. and in 1856 became E. Remington & Sons. In 1888 became Remington Arms Co., 1910 became Remington Arms U.M.C. Co., and finally in 1925 again became Remington Arms Co. Manufacturers of all types of sporting arms.

REMO — Tradename used by Gebruder Rempt of Suhl, Germany before WW-II on rifles.

RENARD — Tradename of Echave y Arizmendi on pistols.

RETRIEVER — Tradename on revolvers from Thomas Ryan, ca. 1870.

REVELATION — Tradename used on sporting arms made for Western Auto Stores.

REV-O-NOC — Tradename used by Hibbard-Spencer-Bartlett Co. of Chicago, Ill. on shotguns made by Crescent Fire Arms Co.

REX — Tradename used by Gregorio Bolumburu on pistols.

RF — Tradename used by Rohm on revolvers.

RG — Abbreviation for Rohm Gesellschaft on guns from West Germany, in the U.S. on guns made by RG Industries following the German pattern.

RG INDUSTRIES — Manufacturer of handguns in Miami, Fla. on the pattern of guns made by Rohm Gesellschaft of West Germany.

RHEINMETALL — Tradename of Rheinische Metallwaren Fabrik.

RHODE ISLAND ARMS CO. — Manufacturer of Morrone shotguns in Hope Valley, R.I. from 1948 to 1953.

R.I.C. — Abbreviation for Royal Irish Constabulary on Webley revolvers.

RICHARDS, W. — Tradename on Belgian shotguns imported about 1900.

RICHLAND ARMS CO. — Importers in Blissfield, Mich. since 1973.

RICHTER, CHARLES — Tradename on shotguns made for New York Sporting Goods Co. by Crescent Fire Arms Co.

RICKARD ARMS — Tradename of J.A. Rickard Co. of Schenectady, N.Y. on shotguns made by Crescent Fire Arms Co.

RIEDL, JAMES — Manufacturer of single shot rifles in San Juan Capistrano, Calif. since 1972.

RINO GALESI — Tradename of Rigarmi, used on pistols.

RIOT — Tradename used by J. Stevens Arms Co. on shotguns.

RIVAL — Tradename on rifles made by Manufrance.

RIVAL — Tradename used by Van Camp Hardware of Indianapolis, Indiana on shotguns made by Crescent Fire Arms Co.

RIVERSIDE ARMS CO. — Tradename used by Stevens Arms & Tool Co.

rln — WW-II German ordnance code assigned to Karl Zeiss, Jena.

RM — Abbreviation on Italian military arms meaning Regia Marina (Royal Navy).

RMAC — Tradename and abbreviation of Rocky Mountain Arms Co.

ROB ROY — Tradename on revolvers from Hood Firearms Co., ca. 1880.

ROBAR ET DE KIRHOVE — Arms makers in Liege, Belgium starting about 1920. In 1927 became L. Robar, in 1933 Robar & Co., in 1948 Societe Robar et Cie until about 1959.

ROBIN HOOD — Tradename used by Hood Firearms Co. on revolvers, ca. 1880.

ROCHESTER DEFENCE CORP. — Predecessor to National Postal Meter in Rochester, NY, manufacturer of M-1 carbines during WW-II.

ROCK-OLA MFG. CO. — Manufacturer of M-1 carbines in Chicago, Ill. during WW-II.

ROHM GESELLSCHAFT — Current manufacturer of handguns in Sontheim/Brenz, West Germany. Imported into the U.S. under many tradenames, and with some models being made now by RG Industries in the U.S.

ROLAND — Tradename of Francisco Arizmendi.

ROMANSKI, B. — Current manufacturer of target arms in Oberndorf, West Germany.

ROME REVOLVER AND NOVELTY WORKS — Makers of revolvers in Rome, N.Y., ca. 1880.

ROMO — Tradename used on Rohm revolvers.

ROSCO — "Rosco Arms Co." marked on Rohm revolvers that are also marked "Vestpocket."

ROSSI, MAEDEO S.A. — Sao Leopoldo, Brazil from about 1965, manufacturer of sporting arms.

ROUTLEDGE MFG. CO. — Small arms maker in Monroe, Mich., ca. 1950.

ROWEN, BECKER CO. — Manufacturer of M-1 carbines in Waterville, Ohio, ca. 1948.

ROYAL — Tradename on revolvers possibly from Hopkins & Allen, ca. 1880.

ROYAL — Tradename of Zulaica y Cia. on pistols.

ROYAL GUN CO. — Tradename used by Three Barrel Gun Co. of Wheeling, W. Va., ca. 1906 on shotguns.

ROYAL SERVICE — Tradename used by Shapleigh Hardware Co. of St. Louis, Mo.

RUBI — Tradename on pistols from Etablecimientos Venturini in South America.

RUBY — Generic term applied to the standard pattern of French WW-I pistols in .32 ACP caliber manufactured under license from Gabilondo y Cia. in Spain.

RUBY — Tradename of Gabilondo y Cia. and used on pistols and revolvers.

RUGER — See Sturm, Ruger & Co.

RUMMEL — Tradename of A.J. Rummel Arms Co. of Toledo, Ohio on shotguns from Crescent Fire Arms Co.

RUPERTUS, JACOB — Also known as Rupertus Pat'd. Pistol Mfg. Co. from 1858 to 1899. Made various types of handguns in Philadelphia, Pa.

RWS — Abbreviation for Rheinische-Westfalische Sprengstoff, cartridge makers since 1931 in various cities in Germany.

RYAN, THOMAS — Manufacturer of revolvers in Norwich, Conn. 1890-93.

S

s — WW-II German ordnance code assigned to Dynamit AG (A. Nobel & Co.), Lumbrays plant.

SABOTTI & TANFOGLIO FABBRICA D'ARMI — Manufacturer of SATA pistols in Brescia, Italy. Reported out of business 1958.

S.A.C.M. — Abbreviation for Soc. Alsacienne de Constructions Mecaniques.

SACO — Abbreviation and tradename of Security Arms Co. of Arlington, Va., importers.

SAFETY POLICE — Tradename used by Hopkins & Allen on revolvers, ca. 1890.

S.A.G.E.M. — Abbreviation for Soc. de Applications General Electriques et Mecaniques.

SAGINAW STEERING GEAR — A division of General Motors that manufactured M-1 carbines in Saginaw and Grand Rapids, Mich. during WW-II.

SANDERSON'S — Importers in Portage, Wisc.

SANNA — Tradename of Dan Pienaar Enterprises of Johannesburg, South Africa on machine pistols.

SANTA BARBARA — Tradename of Santa Barbara of America, Inc. of Irving, Tx. on rifles made by La Caruna Arsenal in Spain.

SANTA MONICA GUNS — Custom rifle makers in Santa Monica, Calif., ca. 1950.

SARASQUETA, VICTOR — Sporting arms manufacturer in Eibar, Spain from 1934.

SARMCO — Importer of sporting arms in Seattle, Wash., ca. 1970.

SATA — Tradename of Sabotti & Tanfoglio Fabbrica d'Armi on pistols.

SATURN — Tradename of custom rifles made by Santa Monica Guns, Santa Monica, Calif., ca. 1950.

SAUER, J.P. & SOHN — Manufacturer of sporting and military arms established in Suhl, Germany in 1751. Now located in Eckenforde, West Germany.

SAVAGE ARMS CORP. — Established in 1893 in Utica, N.Y. as Savage Repeating Arms Co. In 1899 was renamed Savage Arms Co. and in 1917 was incorporated and called Savage Arms Corp. The firm is now in Westfield, Mass. and controls J. Stevens Arms Co., Springfield Arms Co., and A.H. Fox.

S.B.A. — Abbreviation for Santa Barbara Arms on Mauser type rifle actions.

SCHILLING, V.C. — Military arms and sporting rifle manufacturer in Suhl, Germany.

SCHILLING, V. CHARLES — Manufacturer of Bergmann pistols in Suhl, Germany. Also produced sporting and military arms.

SCHMIDT & HABERMAN — Sporting arms makers in Suhl, Germany 1920-40.

SCHULTZ & LARSEN — Sporting arms makers in Otterup, Denmark.

SCHWARZLOSE — Pistol and machine gun manufacturer in Linsenplatz, Germany 1911-27.

SCHWEIZERISCHE INDUSTRIE GESELLSCHAFT — See S.I.G.

SCOTT ARMS CO. — Tradename on revolvers probably from the Norwich Falls Pistol Co., ca. 1880.

SCOTT REVOLVER-RIFLE — Tradename used by Hopkins & Allen on long barreled revolvers, ca. 1880.

SCOTT, W. & C. — Military and sporting arms makers in London and Birmingham, England from 1853 until they merged with P. Webley & Son to form Webley & Scott in 1898.

SCOUT — Tradename used by Frankfurt Hardware of Milwaukee, Wisc. on revolvers made by Hood Firearms, ca. 1870.

SCOUT — Tradename used by J. Stevens Arms Co. on shotguns.

S.E.A.M. — Abbreviation for Soc. Espanola de Armas y Municiones.

SEARS — Tradename on firearms made for Sears, Roebuck & Co. by various makers.

SECOURS — Tradename of Tomas de Urizar y Cia.

SECRET SERVICE SPECIAL — Tradename used by the Fred Bifflar Co. of Chicago, Ill. on revolvers made by Iver Johnson and by Meriden Firearms Co.

SECURITY INDUSTRIES OF AMERICA — Current manufacturer of revolvers in Little Ferry, N.J.

SEDGLEY, R.F., INC. — Successor to Henry M. Kolb, maker of "Baby Hammerless" revolvers in 1910 in Philadelphia, Pa. Also made sporting rifles, and ceased operations in 1938.

SELECTA — Tradename on pistols used by Echave y Arizmendi (Spain).

SELECTA — Tradename on pistols used by Mre. d'Armes des Pyrenees (France).

SENIORITA — Tradename used by Rohm on revolvers.

SERVICE ARMAMENT CO. — Founded in 1957 by Val J. Forgett, Jr. as importers of surplus military arms and ammunition. They now import Webley & Scott shotguns, Fiocchi Ammunition, and collector's guns. Also see Navy Arms, Classic Arms.

S.F.M. — Abbreviation for Soc. Francaise des Munitions de Chasse et de Tir of St. Etienne, France.

S & H — Abbreviation for Sharpe & Hart, importers in Emmitsburg, Md., ca. 1960.

SHADOW — Tradename used on shotguns made in Japan by Nikko Arms Co. Ltd.

SHARPE & HART — Importer of Schultz & Larsen rifles in Emmitsburg, Md., ca. 1960, later called Philip B. Sharpe Associates, ca. 1965.

SHARP'S ARMS CO. — Manufacturer of replica Sharp's rifles in Salt Lake City, Utah 1969 until purchased by Colt in 1970.

SHARPSHOOTER — Tradename used on pistols by Hijos de Calixto Arrizabalaga.

SHATTUCK, C.S. ARMS CO. — Hatfield, Mass. 1880 to 1910. Makers of revolvers, palm pistols, and shotguns.

SHEFFIELD — Tradename used by A. Baldwin & Co. of New Orleans, La., ca. 1900.

SHERIDAN PRODUCTS, INC. — Manufacturer of single-shot pistols in Racine, Wisc. 1953-60.

SHIKAR — Tradename used by Voere on rifles.

SHILEN RIFLES, INC. — Current rifle and barrel maker in Ennis, Texas.

SHILOH PRODUCTS — Current makers of reproduction Sharp's Rifles in Farmingdale, N.Y.

SHORTY — Tradename used by Rohm on revolvers.

SHUE'S SPECIAL — Tradename used by Ira M. Shue Co. of Hanover, Pa., ca. 1900.

SICKEL'S ARMS CO. — Tradename used by Robert Sickels & Preston Co., Davenport, Iowa on shotguns imported from Belgium.

S.I.G. — Abbreviation for Schweizerische Industrie Gesellschaft in Neuhasen, Switzerland since 1857. Manufacturer of all types of sporting and military arms.

SILE DISTRIBUTORS — Current importers in N.Y.C.

SIMPLEX — Model of Bergmann pistol that was made by several firms.

SIMPSON — Tradename on revolvers made by Iver Johnson for J.P. Lovell & Co. of Boston, Mass.

SIMSON & CO. — Suhl, Germany 1910-39, makers of bayonets, rifles, and pistols. Also known as Waffenfabrik Simson.

SINGER — Tradename on pistols used by Arizmendi y Goenaga.

660 — WW-II German ordnance code assigned to Steyr-Daimler-Puch AG, Steyr, Austria.

skd — WW-II German ordnance code assigned to Selve-Kornbiegel-Dornheim AG, Suhl plant, Germany.

SKB — Current manufacturer of sporting arms in Japan.

SLAVIA — Tradename on pistols from A. Vilimek.

SLOAN'S SPORTING GOODS — Importer formerly of New York City, now in Ridgefield, Conn. Tradenames include Charles Daly and P.O.S.

S - M CORP. — Abbreviation for Sydney Manson Corp., manufacturer of single-shot pistols in Alexandria, Va.

S. MFG. CO. — Tradename of Singer Manufacturing Co. of Elizabeth, N.J. on M1911A1 pistols made in 1942.

SMFM — Abbreviation for Societe de Fab. Mech. of St. Etienne, France. Manufacturer of electrically fired guns, cal. 1965.

SMITH, OTIS A. — Manufacturer of revolvers 1873-90 in Middlefield and Rockfall, Conn.

SMOKER — Tradename on revolvers from Johnson, Bye & Co., ca. 1875.

SMOKEY CITY — Tradename on revolvers made by Iver Johnson for J.P. Lovell of Boston, Mass.

SOCIETE ROBAR ET CIE. — See Robar et De Kirhove.

SODIA, FRANZ — Manufacturer of sporting arms in Ferlach, Austria since 1934.

SOLINGEN CUTLERY — Importers in Montrose, Calif. of German revolvers, ca. 1970.

SOSSO, GIULLIO — Pistol designer in Turin, Italy, later pistols made by Fabb. Nazionale Armi in Brescia, Italy.

SOUTHERN ARMS CO. — Tradename used by H & D Folsom Co. on shotguns made by Crescent Fire Arms Co.

SPECIAL SERVICE — Tradename used on shotguns made by Crescent Fire Arms Co. for Shapleigh Hdw. Co.

SPENCER ARMS CO. — Windsor, Conn., ca. 1887, makers of repeating shotguns.

SPENCER GUN CO. — Tradename used by Hibbard & Spencer Bartlett on shotguns made by Crescent Fire Arms Co.

SPENCER REPEATING RIFLE CO. — Boston, Mass. from 1862 until it was purchased by Winchester Repeating Arms Co. in 1869. Spencer was also associated with the Roper Repeating Rifle Co. which for a time made the Spencer-Roper Shotgun.

SPENCER SAFETY HAMMERLESS — Tradename used by the Columbia Armory, Columbia, Tenn. on revolvers, ca. 1892.

SPESCO CORP. — Importers of firearms located in Atlanta, Ga. since about 1970.

SPORTCO — Tradename used by Omark Australia Ltd. of St. Marys, South Australia on sporting arms.

SPORTSMAN — Tradename used by J. Stevens Arms Co. on Model 315 and Model 90 shotguns.

SPORTSMAN — Tradename used by W. Bingham Co. of Cleveland, Ohio on shotguns made by Crescent Fire Arms Co.

SPRINGFIELD — U.S. Government armory that manufactured military arms in Springfield, Mass. from 1782.

SPRINGFIELD ARMS — Tradename used by Crescent Fire Arms Co. on shotguns.

SPRINGFIELD ARMS CO. — Sporting arms manufacturer in Springfield, Mass. since 1851, and is now part of Savage Arms Corp.

SPRINTER — Tradename used by Garate Anitua y Cia. of Eibar, Spain on pistols.

SPY — Tradename used by Norwich Falls Pistol Co. on revolvers, ca. 1880.

SQUARE DEAL — Tradename used by Stratton-Warren Hdw. Co. of Memphis, Tenn. on shotguns made by Crescent Fire Arms Co.

SQUIBMAN — Tradename on arms made by Squires Bingham of the Philippines, imported by Century Arms.

SQUIRES BINGHAM — Current makers of sporting arms in Makati, Rizal, Philippines.

S & S — Tradename and abbreviation of J.P. Sauer & Sohn.

SS-25 — Tradename on pistols made by Bar-Sto Precision in Burbank, Calif., ca. 1973.

STAFFS-BILT — Tradename of Staggs Enterprises in Phoenix, Arizona, ca. 1970.

STAKE, T.W. — Reported to be tradename of Schoverling, Daly, & Gales of New York City, ca. 1900.

STALLION — Tradename on revolvers imported by J.L. Galef & Son.

STANDARD ARMS CO. — Manufacturer of rifles in Wilmington, Del. 1909-11.

STANDARD PRODUCTS CO. — Manufacturer of M-1 carbines during WW-II in Port Clinton, Ohio.

STANLEY — Tradename on shotguns imported from Belgium, ca. 1900.

STAR — Tradename of Bonafacio Echeverria.

STAR GAUGE — Tradename used by Interarms on shotguns imported from Spain.

STATE ARMS CO. — Tradename used by J.H. Lau & Co. of New York City on shotguns made by Crescent Fire Arms Co.

STERLING ARMS CORP. — Manufacturer of pistols and rifles, established 1968 in Buffalo, N.Y. In 1973 purchased by E. & R. Machine and moved to Gasport, N.Y., 1978 moved to Lockport, N.Y.

STERLING ARMS CORP. — Tradename used by H & D Folsom Co. on shotguns made by Crescent Fire Arms Co.

STENDA WERKE WAFFENBAU — Makers of the Beholla pistol from about 1920 to the mid-1920's.

STERN — Tradename on pistols used by Albin Wahl.

STEVENS, J. ARMS & TOOL CO. — Established in 1864 in Chicopee Falls, Mass. Absorbed Page-Lewis Arms Co., Davis-Warner Arms Co., and Crescent Fire Arms Co. in 1926, and was in turn absorbed by Savage Arms Corp. in 1936.

ST. HUBERT — Tradename of Mre. d'Armes des Pyrenees.

STINGRAY — Tradename on .25 acp pistols used by Hy Hunter on guns imported from Germany, ca. 1960.

ST. LOUIS ARMS CO. — Tradename used by Shapleigh Hardware Co. of St. Louis, Mo. on shotguns made by Crescent Fire Arms Co.

STOEGER INDUSTRIES — Manufacturer and importer established in N.Y.C. 1924, now located in South Hackensack, N.J.

STOSEL — Tradename used by Retolaza Hermanos.

STRIKER — Tradename used by Hopkins & Allen on revolvers, ca. 1870.

STUKA — Tradename used by Hy Hunter of Burbank, Calif. on imported pistols, ca. 1960.

STURM, RUGER & CO. — Manufacturer of sporting arms in Southport, Conn.

ST. W. — Abbreviation for Stenda Werke.

SULLIVAN ARMS CO. — Tradename used by Sullivan Hdw. in Anderson, S.C. on shotguns made by Crescent Fire Arms Co.

SUPER DESTROYER — Tradename used by Gaztanaga, Trocaola y Ibarzabal on pistols.

SUPER DREADNAUGHT — Tradename used by J. Stevens Arms Co. on shotguns.

SUPER RANGE GOOSE — Tradename used by J. Stevens Arms Co.

SUPER RANGER — Tradename used by Sears, Roebuck & Co.

svw — WW-II German ordnance code assigned to Mauser-Werke, Oberndorf on the Neckar, Germany.

S & W — Abbreviation for Smith & Wesson. 57

SWAMP ANGEL — Tradename used

by Forehand & Wadsworth on revolvers, ca. 1872.

SWIFT — Tradename used on revolvers by Iver Johnson, ca. 1900.

SWIFT DA. — Tradename used by Hopkins & Allen on revolvers made for J.P. Lovel of Boston, Mass., ca. 1900.

SWIFT RIFLE CO. — Manufacturer of military arms in London, ca. 1943.

swp — WW-II German ordnance code assigned to Waffenwerke Brunn AG, Brunn, Czechoslovakia.

SYCO — Tradename used by Wyeth Hardware of St. Joseph, Mo.

SYMPATHIQUE — Tradename on pistols from Mre. d'Armes des Pyrenees.

T

t — WW-II German ordnance code assigned to Dynamit AG, Troisdorf plant.

ta — WW-II German ordnance code assigned to Durener Metallwerke, AG, Berlin-Borsigwalde, Germany.

TAC — Tradename on carbines made by Demro Products of Manchester, Conn. (formerly Foxco).

T.A.C. — Abbreviation for Trucaola, Aranzabal y Cia.

TALA — Tradename used by Tallares de Armas Livianas Argentinas.

TALLARES ARMAS LIVIANAS ARGENTINAS — Manufacturer of pistols in Punta Alta, Argentina.

TANARMI — Tradename on pistols imported by Excam.

TANQUE — Tradename on guns made for Ojanguren y Vidosa.

TARGA — Tradename used by Excam on Italian pistols, ca. 1976.

TARN — Tradename on pistols made by Swift Rifle Co. in London, England, ca. 1943.

TAULER — Tradename used by Tauler of Madrid, Spain on pistols made by Gabilondo y Cia. of Elgoibar, Spain.

TAURUS — Tradename for Forjas Taurus S.A. of P. Alegre, Brazil on revolvers currently manufactured.

TDA — Tradename on Thermodynamic Systems revolvers distributed by E.M.F. of Studio City, Calif.

TDE MARKETING CORP. — Maker of AutoMag and Backup pistols in South El Monte, Calif.

TECHNI-MEC — Tradename on shotguns currently made by Fabbrica d'Armi di Isidoro Rizzini of Brescia, Italy.

TED WILLIAMS — Tradename used by Sears, Roebuck & Co. on rifles and shotguns from various makers.

TEN STAR — Tradename used on imported Belgian shotguns, ca. 1900 for Geller, Ward & Hasner of St. Louis, Mo.

TERRIBLE — Tradename on pistols from Hijos de Calixto Arrizabalaga.

TERRIER — Tradename used on revolvers by Tryon Bros., guns made by J. Rupertus, ca. 1880.

TERROR — Tradename on revolvers from Forehand & Wadsworth, ca. 1870.

TEUF-TEUF — Tradename on pistols made by Arizmendi y Goenaga of Eibar, Spain and should not be confused with the Belgian guns with a similar name.

TEXAS RANGER — Tradename used by J. Stevens Arms Co. on single shot shotguns for Montgomery Ward & Co.

T.G.E. — Abbreviation for Tokyo Gas & Electric, used on Baby Nambu pistols.

THALCO — Tradename on Rohm revolvers.

THALMAN-WERK, ERNST VEB — Manufacturer of sporting arms in Suhl, Germany since 1945. Successor to C.G. Haenel.

THAMES ARMS CO. — Makers of double action revolvers in Norwich, Conn., ca. 1907, possibly tradename of H & A or H & R. Also reported to be tradename used by Charles J. Godfrey of N.Y.C.

THAYER, ROBINSON & CARY — Makers of double action revolvers in Norwich, Conn., ca. 1907.

THERMODYNAMIC SYSTEMS — Tradename on revolvers distributed by E.M.F. of Studio City, Calif.

THOMPSON AUTOMATICS — See Auto Ordnance.

THOMPSON/CENTER ARMS CO. — Current manufacturer of handguns and blackpowder arms in Rochester, N.H.

THUNDER — Tradename used by M. Bascaran on pistols.

THUNDERBIRD — Model of Cody Mfg. Corp. revolver.

TIGER — Tradename used by J.H. Hall Co. of Nashville, Tenn. on shotguns made by Crescent Fire Arms Co.

TIGRE — Tradename on pistols by Garate, Anitua y Cia.

TIKKA — Tradename on rifles made by Oy Tikkakoski.

TINGLE MFG. CO. — Manufacturer of blackpowder arms in Shelbyville, Ind. since about 1960.

TITAN — Tradename used on pistols made by Tanfoglio Giuseppi in Brescia, Italy, and imported by E.I.G. before 1968. Now made in the U.S. by F.I.E.

TITAN — Tradename of Retolaza Hermanos on pistols (Spain).

TITANIC — Tradename of Retolaza Hermanos on pistols.

TOBIN ARMS CO. — Shotgun manufacturer in Norwich, Conn. from 1905-09, and in Woodstock, Ontario, Canada from 1910-23.

TOBIN SIMPLEX — Tradename used by Tobin Arms Co.

TOKAGYPT — Tradename used on pistols made for the Egyptian army by Femaru Fegyver es Gepgyar of Budapest, Hungary.

TOMMA — Tradename on 4-barrel

pistols made by H.D.H., in Liege, Belgium, and also by an unknown firm in Germany, ca. 1920.

TOMPKINS — Tradename on pistols made by Varsity Mfg. Co. of Springfield, Mass., ca. 1947.

TORKELSON ARMS CO. — Shotgun makers in Warren, Mass. from 1903-08.

TOURISTE — Tradename used by Mre. d'Armes des Pyrenees on pistols.

TOWER'S POLICE SAFETY — Tradename used by Hopkins & Allen on revolvers, ca. 1875.

TOWNLEY'S PAL — Tradename used by Townley Hardware Co., Kansas City, Mo., ca. 1900.

TOZ — Tradename of Tulski Oruzheinyi Zavod on pistols.

TRADEWINDS — Importers in Tacoma, Wash. from about 1954 to 1974.

TRAMP'S TERROR — Tradename used by Hood Firearms Co. on revolvers, ca. 1880.

TRAPS BEST — Tradename used by Watkins-Cottrell Co. of Richmond, Va.

TREJO — See Armas Trejo, A.A.

TRIDENT — Tradename on Colt type revolvers made in South Africa by Induna.

TRIOMPHE — Tradename on pistols from Apaolozo Hermanos.

TRIOMPHE FRANCAISE — Tradename used by Mre. d'Armes des Pyrenees.

TRIPLE S DEVELOPMENT CO. — Manufacturer of rifles and shotgun chokes in Wickliffe, Ohio since 1974.

TRIPLEX — Tradename of Domingo Acha on pistols.

TRIUMPH — Tradename used by J. Stevens Arms Co. on shotguns.

TRUE BLUE — Tradename used by Norwich Falls Pistol Co. on revolvers, ca. 1880.

TRUST SUPRA — Tradename used by Garate-Anitua y Cia. on pistols.

T-62 — Tradename used by Hy Hunter of Burbank, Calif. on pistols, ca. 1960.

TUE-TUE — Tradename used by Galand Arms Co. on revolvers.

TURNER & ROSS — Tradename on revolvers made by Hood Firearms Co., ca. 1875.

237 — WW-II German ordnance code assigned to Mauser-Werke, Oberndorf on the Neckar, Germany.

27 — WW-II German ordnance code assigned to B. Geipel GmbH, Waffenfabrik Erma, Erfurt, Germany.

TYCOON — Tradename used by Johnson, Bye & Co. on revolvers, ca. 1875.

T.Y.E. — Abbreviation of Tomas de Urizar y Cia. of Eibar, Spain.

TYROL SPORTING ARMS CO. — Importers in the early 1960's in St. Albans, Vt., until 1968.

U

ua — WW-II German ordnance code assigned to Osnabrucker Kupfer- u. Drahtwerke AG, Osnabruck.

U.A.E. — Abbreviation for Union Armera Eibaressa.

UBERTO, ALDO & C. — Current manufacturer of sporting arms in Ponte Zanano, Italy. Best known for their single action colt type revolvers.

UHLINGER, W.L. & CO. — Philadelphia, Pa., ca. 1880, manufacturer of revolvers.

UMA JAGD U. SPORTWAFFEN FABRIK — Manufacturer of sporting arms in Munich, West Germany since 1975.

U.M.C. — Abbreviation for Union Metallic Cartridge Co.

U.M.C. ARMS CO. — Tradename on revolvers probably used by Norwich Falls Pistol Co., ca. 1880. Not to be confused with U.M.C.

UNBRAUCHBAR — West German rejection mark on gun parts, means "useless."

U-9 — Tradename of rifles made for Herters, Inc. by B.S.A.

UNCETA Y ESPERANZA — See Astra.

UNCLE SAM — Tradename used by Iver Johnson, and also by J. Palmer O'Neal Co. of Pittsburgh, Pa.

UNDERWOOD-ELLIOT-FISHER CO. Manufacturer of M-1 carbines during WW-II at Hartford, Conn.

UNION — Tradename used by Fabrique a St. Etienne on long gripped .25 acp pistols (France).

UNION ARMS CO. — See Union Firearms Co.

UNION FIREARMS CO. — Toledo, Ohio from 1903 until purchased by Ithaca Gun Co. in 1913. Manufacturer of shotguns and unusual revolvers. Also known as Union Arms Co.

UNION JACK — Tradename on revolvers made by Hood Firearms Co., ca. 1880.

UNION METALLIC CARTRIDGE CO. — Established in 1886 in Bridgeport, Conn., manufacturer of ammunition and powder flasks. Merged with Remington Arms Co. in 1902.

UNION I — Tradename used on .25 acp pistols made for Esperanza y Unceta (Spain).

UNIQUE — Tradename used by C.S. Shattuck on revolvers, ca. 1880.

UNIQUE — Tradename used by Mre. d'Armes des Pyrenees on sporting arms.

UNIS — Tradename used by Mre. d'Armes des Pyrenees (France).

UNIS — Tradename used by Santigo Salaberrin (Spain).

UNITED STATES ARMS CORP. — Manufacturer of revolvers in Riverhead, N.Y. since 1976.

UNIVERSAL SPORTING GOODS, INC. — Hialeah, Fla. since 1964, manufacturer of M-1 carbines and their variations, and importer of Russian shotguns.

UN-QUALITY — Marking on receivers of M-1 carbines made during WW-II by Union Switch & Signal and assembled by Underwood-Elliot-Fisher.

U.S. ARMS & CUTLERY CO. — Rochester, N.Y., ca. 1876, manufacturer of knife pistols and unusual arms.

U.S. ARMS CO. — Brooklyn, N.Y. 1874-78, manufacturer of revolvers.

U.S. ARMS CO. — New York City 1874-78, manufacturer of knife pistols and revolvers.

U.S. ARMS CO. — Tradename on shotguns made for H & D Folsom Co. by Crescent Fire Arms Co.

U.S. REVOLVER CO. — Tradename used by Iver Johnson on revolvers.

U. S. & S. — Tradename and abbreviation for Union Switch & Signal of Swissvale, Pa. on M1911A1 pistols made in 1943.

U.S. SMALL ARMS CO. — Chicago, Ill., ca. 1917, manufacturer of knife pistols.

V

va — WW-II German ordnance code assigned to Kabel- u. Metallwerke Neumeyer AG, Nurnberg, Germany.

VAINQUER — Tradename used by Aurelio Mendiola.

VALIANT — Tradename used by J. Stevens Arms Co. on rifles made for Spear & Co. of Pittsburgh, Pa.

VALOR IMPORTS CORP. — Current importer in Hialeah, Fla.

VALTION KIVAARI TEHDAS — Jyvaskyla, Finland (State Rifle Factory). In 1935 they manufactured the Lahti pistol.

VAP — Tradename and abbreviation of Vapen Specialists AB of Stockholm, Sweden since 1957. Manufacturer of free rifles.

VARSITY MFG. CO. — Manufacturer of Tompkins pistols, ca. 1947 in Springfield, Mass.

V.B. — Abbreviation of Vincenzo Bernardelli on pistols.

V.C.S. — Abbreviation for V. Charles Schilling on pistols.

ve — WW-II German ordnance code assigned to Cartoucherie de Valence.

VEB FAHRZEUG U. GERATEWERK SIMSON — Current manufacturer of sporting arms in Suhl, East Germany.

VEGA — Manufacturer of M1911 frames in Sacramento, Calif. since about 1976.

VENCEDOR — Tradename used by San Martin y Cia. on pistols.

VENTURA IMPORTS — Current importers of shotguns in Seal Beach, Calif.

VENUS — Tradename on pistols from Tomas de Urizar y Cia.

VER-CAR — Tradename of Verney-Carron.

VERNEY-CARRON — Current sporting arms manufacturer in St. Etienne, France.

VESTA — Tradename of Hijos de A. Echeverria.

VETERAN — Tradename used by Norwich Falls Pistol Co. on revolvers, ca. 1880.

VESTPOCKET — Tradename found on Rohm revolvers marked "Rosco Arms Co."

VICTOR — Tradename on pistols from Francisco Arizmendi.

VICTOR — Tradename used on shotguns made by Crescent Fire Arms Co.

VICTOR #1 — Tradename used by Harrington & Richardson on revolvers, ca. 1876.

VICTOR SPECIAL — Tradename used by Hibbard-Spencer-Bartlett Co. of Chicago on shotguns made by Crescent Fire Arms Co.

VICTORIA — Tradename of pistols from Esperanza y Unceta (Astra).

VICTORIA — Tradename on revolvers manufactured by Hood Firearms Co., ca. 1880.

VINCITOR — Tradename of pistols from M. Zulaica y Cia.

VINDEX — Tradename used by Mre. d'Armes des Pyrenees.

VIRGINIA ARMS CO. — Tradename used by Virginia-Caroline Co. of Richmond, Va. on shotguns made by Crescent Fire Arms Co.

VIRGINIAN — Tradename on single action revolvers made by Hammerli of Switzerland, and now by Interarms in Virginia.

VITE — Tradename of Echave & Arizmendi of Eibar, Spain on pistols, ca. 1913.

VKT — Tradename and abbreviation for Valtion Kivaari Tehdas on Finnish Lahtis (Jyvaskyca, Fin.).

V.L. & D. — Abbreviation for Von Lengerke & Detmold importers in N.Y.C. from the turn of the century until purchased by Abercrombie & Fitch.

VOERE — Current sporting arms manufacturer in Kufstein, Austria.

VOLUNTEER — Tradename used by J. Stevens Arms Co. on shotguns for Belknap Hdw. Co. of Louisville, Ky.

VOM HOFE — Tradename currently used by W. Gehmann of Karlsruhe & Stuttgart, West Germany, named for originator of Vom Hofe Calibers, ca. 1937.

VON LENGERKE & DETMOLD — See V.L. & D.

VULCAN ARMS CO. — Tradename used on shotguns manufactured by Crescent Fire Arms Co.

vzg — WW-II German ordnance code assigned to Vereinigte Zunder- u. Kabelwerke, Meissen, Germany.

W

w — WW-II German ordnance code assigned to Gesellschaft zur Verwertung Chem. Erzeugnisse, Wolfratshausen plant.

wa — WW-II German ordnance code assigned to Hasag, Hugo Schneider

AG, Lampenfabrik, Leipzig, Germany.

WAC — Abbreviation for Winfield Arms Corp., importers in Los Angeles, Calif. in the late 1950's, and Western Arms Corp. in the early 1950's.

W.A.C. — Abbreviation for Warner Arms Corp. on Schwarzlose pistols, ca. 1911.

WAFFENFABRIK MAUSER — See Mauser Werke Ag.

WAFFENFABRIK SIMSON — See Simson & Co.

WAFFEN FRANKONIA — Current manufacturer and distributor in Wurzburg, W. Germany.

WAHL, ALBIN — Pistol maker in Zella-Mehlis, Germany.

WALAM — Tradename on copies of the Walther PP made by Femaru Fegyver es Gepgyar in Budapest, Hungary.

WALDMAN — Tradename used by Francisco Arizmendi.

WALTHER, CARL — Manufacturer of sporting and military arms since 1886 in Zella-Mehlis, Germany until 1945, and now in Ulm, West Germany.

WAMO MFG. CO. — Manufacturer of pistols from about 1956 to 1959 in San Gabriel, Calif.

WARREN ARMS CORP. — Tradename used on shotguns imported from Belgium, ca. 1900.

WASP — Tradename on pistols from Hawes, ca. 1970.

WATSON BROS. — Sporting arms makers in London, England 1885-1931.

WAUTAUGA — Tradename used by Wallace Hardware Co. of Morristown, Tenn.

wb — WW-II German ordnance code assigned to Hasag, Berlin, Germany.

wc — WW-II German ordnance code assigned to Hasag, Hugo Schneider AG, Meuselwitz plant, Thuringia, Germany.

wd — WW-II German ordnance code assigned to Hasag, Hugo Schneider AG, Taucha plant.

we — WW-II German ordnance code assigned to Hasag, Hugo Schneider AG, Langewiesen plant.

WEATHERBY'S — Manufacturer and importer of rifles and shotguns in South Gate, Calif. since about 1947.

WEIHRAUCH, HERMAN SPORTWAFFENFABRIK — Manufacturers of handguns in Mellrichstadt/Bayern, West Germany.

WESSON FIREARMS CO. — Manufacturers of shotguns in Springfield, Mass. 1864-68.

WESSON, FRANK — Worcester, Mass. 1854 to 1865, then moved to Springfield, Mass. Produced military and sporting arms until 1875.

WESSON & HARRINGTON — Worcester, Mass. 1871-74, manufacturer of revolvers. Succeeded by Harrington & Richardson.

WESTERN ARMS CO. — New York City, ca. 1870, maker of revolvers.

WESTERN FIELD — Tradename used by Montgomery Ward on rifles and shotguns.

WESTERN GUN EXCHANGE — Importers of German shotguns in Whittier, Calif., ca. 1950.

WESTERN LONG RANGE — Tradename used by Ithaca Gun Co. on shotguns.

WESTERN STYLE — Tradename found on Rohm revolvers.

wf — WW-II German ordnance code assigned to Hasag, Hugo Schneider AG, Kielce plant, Poland.

wg — WW-II German ordnance code assigned to Hasag, Hugo Schneider AG, Altenburg plant.

wh — WW-II German ordnance code assigned to Hasag, Hugo Schneider AG, Eisenach plant.

WHIPPET — Tradename used by J. Stevens Arms Co. on single shot shotguns for Hibbard, Spencer, Bartlett Co. of Chicago, Ill.

WHITE POWDER NITRO — Tradename used by J. Stevens Arms Co. on shotguns.

WHITE POWDER WONDER — Tradename used by Sears, Roebuck & Co. on shotguns.

WHITE POWDER WONDER — Tradename used by J. Stevens Arms Co. on shotguns.

WHITMORE, NATHANIEL G. — Manufacturer of single shot rifles in Eastondale, Mass. 1880 to 1917.

WHITNEY FIREARMS CO. — Makers of the "Whitney Wolverine" pistol in Hartford, Conn. from 1955 to 1962.

WHITNEY SAFETY GUN CO. — Shotgun makers in Florence, Mass., ca. 1893.

WICHITA — Tradename on rifles currently made by Wichita Engineering and Supply, Inc. of Wichita, Kansas.

WICKLIFFE — Tradename of Triple S Development Co. on rifles.

WIDE AWAKE — Tradename used by Hood Firearms on revolvers, ca. 1880.

WILDEY FIREARMS CO. — Manufacturer of gas operated pistols in Cold Spring, N.Y., established in 1975.

WILKINSON ARMS — Manufacturer of the "Diane" pistol in South El Monte, Calif., ca. 1976.

WILKINSON ARMS CO. — Tradename used by Richmond Hardware Co. of Richmond, Va. on shotguns imported from Belgium, ca. 1900.

WILMONT ARMS CO. — Tradename on shotguns imported from Belgium, ca. 1900.

WILSHIRE ARMS CO. — Tradename used by Stauffer, Eshleman & Co. of New Orleans, La.

WILTSHIRE ARMS CO. — Tradename used on shotguns imported from Belgium, ca. 1900.

WINCHESTER REPEATING ARMS CO. — New Haven, Conn. 1857 to date. In 1857 Oliver Winchester reorganized the Volcanic Repeating Arms Co. into the New Haven Arms Co., and in 1866 became Winchester Repeating Arms Co. In 1869 absorbed Fogerty Repeating Rifle Co. and American Rifle Co., the Spencer Repeating Arms Co. in 1870, and

Adirondack Arms Co. in 1874.

WINFIELD ARMS CORP. — See WAC.

WINFIELD ARMS CO. — Tradename used by Crescent Fire Arms Co. on shotguns.

WINFIELD ARMS CO. — Tradename used by Norwich Falls Pistol Co. on revolvers, ca. 1880.

WINOCA ARMS CO. — Tradename used by Jacobi Hardware Co. of Philadelphia, Pa. on shotguns made by Crescent Fire Arms Co.

WINSLOW ARMS CO. — Manufacturers of rifles and shotguns in Venice, Fla., ca. 1970, Osprey, Fla., ca. 1976.

WISCHO — Distributors of sporting arms in Erlangen, West Germany.

WITTES HDW. CO. — Tradename on shotguns made by J. Stevens Arms Co. for Wittes Hdw. of St. Louis, Mo.

wj — WW-II German ordnance code assigned to Hasag, Hugo Schneider AG, Oberweissbach plant.

wk — WW-II German ordnance code assigned to Hasag, Hugo Schneider AG, Schlieben plant.

wn — WW-II German ordnance code assigned to Hasag, Hugo Schneider AG, Dernabach plant, Thuringia, Germany.

WOLVERINE ARMS CO. — Tradename used by Fletcher Hardware Co. of Wilmington, N.C. on shotguns made by Crescent Fire Arms Co.

WORTHINGTON ARMS — Tradename used by J. Stevens Arms Co. on shotguns.

WORTHINGTON ARMS CO. — Tradename used by George Worthington Co. of Cleveland, Ohio on shotguns made by Crescent Fire Arms Co.

WORTHINGTON, GEORGE — See Worthington Arms.

WRA — Abbreviation for Winchester Repeating Arms.

X

xa — WW-II German ordnance code assigned to Busch & Jager, Ludenscheider Metallwerke, Ludenscheid.

XL — Tradename and model name used by Hopkins & Allen, ca. 1890.

XPERT — Tradename used by Hopkins & Allen, ca. 1880.

XX STANDARD — Tradename used by J.M. Marlin on revolvers, ca. 1875.

XXX STANDARD — Tradename used on revolvers by J.M. Marlin, ca. 1875.

Y

y — WW-II German ordnance code assigned to Jagdpatronen, Zundhutchen- u - Metallwarenfabrik AG, Nagyteteny plant, Budapest, Hungary.

ya — WW-II German ordnance code assigned to Sachsische Metallwarenfabrik, August Wellner & Sohn, Aue, Saxony, Germany.

YAMAMOTO FIREARMS — Current shotgun manufacturer in Kochi, Japan.

YDEAL — Tradename used by Francisco Arizmendi.

YOU BET — Tradename used on revolvers by Hopkins & Allen, ca. 1880.

YOUNG AMERICA — Tradename on revolvers made by Harrington & Richardson, ca. 1900.

Z

ZABALA — Manufacturer of shotguns in Spain, imported by Garcia Sporting Arms Corp. of Teaneck, N.J.

ZANOTTI — Arms makers since 1625, now located in Ravenna, Italy.

ZARAGOZA — See Fab. de Armas Zaragoza.

ZAVODI CRVENA ZASTAVIA — Current manufacturer of sporting arms in Belgrade, Yugoslavia.

zb — WW-II German ordnance code assigned to Kupferwerk Ilsenburg AG, Ilsenburg, Harz.

ZCZ — Abbreviation of Zavodi Crvena Zastavia of Belgrade, Yugoslavia.

ZEPHYR — Tradename used by A.F. Stoeger on imported arms, ca. 1960.

ZEPHYR — Tradename on Rohm revolvers.

ZIMMERMANN, HANS — FEINMECHZNIKWAFFEN — Current manufacturer of sporting arms in Oberwildflecken, West Germany.

ZOLI, ANGELO — Current manufacturer of sporting arms in Brescia, Italy.

ZOLI, ANTONIO — Current manufacturer of shotguns in Brescia, Italy.

ZONDA — Tradename used by Hispano Argentina Fab. de Automoviles.

INDEX

Abitua, Etxezaraga y Cia., 2
Acha Hermanos,
Acha, Domingo y Cia, 1, 2
Adler Waffenwerke, 73
Aguirre y Aranzabal, 76
Albin Wahl, Zella-Mehlis, 35
Aldazabal, A., 84
Aldazabal, Jose, 1
Alkartasuna, 17, 41
Alois Tomiska, 1
American Arms Co., 1, 17
American Import Co., 30
Anciens Etablissments Pieper, 32
Andrew Fryberg & Co., 1
Anschutz, J.G., 20, 38
Apaoloza Hermanos, 38, 72
Arana y Cia., 62
Argentinian military mark, 89
Arizaga, Gaspar, 69, 73
Arizmendi y Goenaga, 37, 49, 51, 44
Arizmendi y Zulaica, 26
Arizmendi, Francisco, 20, 37, 67, 72
Armalite, 79
Armand Gavage, 10
Armero Especialistas Reunidas, 1
Armi Famars, 92
Armi Galesi, 17
Armsport, 90
Arostegui, Eulogio, 86
Arostegui, Salvador, 58
Arrizabalaga, Hijos de Calixto, 2, 3
Astra-Unceta y Cia., 35, 61
Austrian proof, 18, 42
Austro-Hungarian proof, 14, 15, 30, 54, 58, 69, 71, 74, 91
Azanza y Arrizabalaga, 13, 33, 51
B.R.F., 41
B.S.A., 92
Barta y Azpiri, 62
Bascaran, Martin A., 21, 36, 37
Bauer Firearms Co., 2
Becker & Hollander, 9
Belgian military mark, 52
Belgian proof, 14, 26, 27, 47, 55, 56, 57, 61, 62, 64, 75, 76, 77
Berasaluze Areitio Aurtena y Cia., 52
Berastain y Cia., 9

Beretta, Pietro, 17, 28, 35, 46
Bergeron, L., 87
Bergmann, Theodor, 17, 26, 32, 42, 50
Berlin-Suhler Waffen, 26
Bernardelli, Vincenzo, 29
Bernardon-Martin, 11
Bernedo y Cia., 17
Bertrand, J., 5, 12, 36
Bestegui Hermanos, 2, 37, 53
Bliss & Goodyear, 90
Bolivian military mark, 88
Bolumburo, Gregorio, 4, 44, 58, 86
Breda, Ernesto, 79
Browning Arms Co., 81
Bulgarian military mark, 88, 89
Burgess Gun Co., 78
Burgsmuller, K., 17
Castelli, 77
Cesar, J., 2
Ceska Zbrojovka, 8, 24
Chilian military mark, 88
Chinese (Republic of) mark, 73
Chinese mark, 61
Clement, Charles Ph., 13, 26, 38
Cody Mfg. Co., 81
Colt, 26, 79
Congolese military mark, 92
Connecticut Valley Arms, 49
Crown City Arms, 53
Crucelegui Hermanos, 2
Czechoslovakian military mark, 88
Czechoslovakian proof, 32, 46, 61, 75, 76, 91
D.W.M., 14, 32, 34
Dakin Gun Co., 49
Danish military mark, 54, 59
Danish proof, 51, 53, 58
Dansk Industri Syndikat, 75
Danzig Arsenal, 53
Dardick Corporation, 30
Davis-Warner Arms, 8
Delu, Fab. d'Armes F., 2
Deutsche Werke, 17
Dictator, 83
Dornheim, G.C., 14, 19, 38, 81
Doyen, Julien, 81
Dusek, F., 17, 30

Dutch Colonial Forces, 4
Dutch military mark, 54, 60
Dutch proof, 60
East German mark, 16, 31,
East German proof, 26, 56, 57, 59, 60, 70, 92, 93
East India Co., 74
Echave y Arizmendi, 11, 18, 25, 26, 36, 77, 82
Echeverria, Bonafacio, 37, 62
Eckoldt, Emil, 26
Egyption mark, 53
EIG Corp., 18
Enfield mark, 14, 55
English Military mark, 45, 46
English proof, 52, 53, 54, 56, 57, 58, 59, 60, 76, 77, 85
Erfurt Arsenal, 55
Erma Werke, 14, 18
Ernesto Breda, 34
Erquiaga, Muguruza, 11
Errasti, Antonio, 13, 55
Esperanza Y Unceta, 2, 27, 29, 53
Esprin Hermanos, 25
Etab. Radarm Fab. d'Armes Liege, 81
Etablissments Darne, 32
Ethiopian military mark, 89
Fab. d'Armes de Grande Precision, 5 12
Fab. d'Armes de Guerre, Eibar, 27
Fab. d'Armes Jannsen et Fils, 4, 46, 73, 80, 83
Fab. d'Armes Unies de Liege, 84
Fab. Material de Guerre, 19
Fab. Nationale d'Armes de Guerre, 35
Fabbrica Nazionale d'Armi, 3
Fabrica de Material de Guerre, 32
Fabrique Nationale, 9, 10, 49, 86
Fabryka Bronn Radom, 31, 70
Fiala, 80
Finland proof, 66, 68, 75
Firearms Import & Export, 3, 18, 41
Firearms International, 18
Firma Pfanni, 9
Forehand & Wadsworth, 37, 78, 92
Franchi, Luigi, 84
Francotte, Auguste, 13, 26, 44, 51
Frank, Adolph, 91

French mark, 16, 33
French Naval mark, 44
French proof, 10, 32, 45, 52, 55, 56 57, 58, 58, 62, 69, 91
Frommer, 9, 83
Funk, Christopher, 31
Gabilondo y Cia., 3, 10, 20, 23, 27, 28, 74, 81, 83, 84
Galef, J.L. & Son, 89
Galesi, 66, 76
Garate, Anitua y Cia., 2, 36, 82
Gasser, L., 87
Gaztanaga, Isidro, 2, 10, 63
Gaztanaga, Trocaola y Ibarzabal, 36
Genschow, Gustav, 15
German 9mm gripmark, 43
German Luftwaffe mark, 72
German military mark, 70, 71
German Nazi mark (NSKK), 72
German Nazi military mark, 72
German Nazi naval mark, 71
German Nazi police mark, 70, 71
German Nazi RZM mark, 23
German proof, 51, 52, 53, 55, 56, 57, 58, 59, 60, 70, 71
German Weimar Naval mark, 44, 71
Gerstenberger u. Eberwein, 18, 21, 24, 25, 65
Gevelot, 38
Gevelot et Gaupillat, 4
Glisenti, 88
Golden Eagle, 72
Gotthilf von Nordheim, 27
Grabner, Georg, 3
Greek military proof, 93
Greifelt & Co., 50
Guatemalan military mark, 93
Guisasola Hermanos, 3, 10
Gustav, Carl, 53
Gustloff Werke, 19
Gwinn Arms Co., 82
Haenel, C.G., 12, 35, 38
Hammerli, 48, 86
Harrington & Richardson, 19, 65, 67, 75, 77, 91
Hawes Firearms, 19, 62
Heckler & Koch, 15
Hege, 79

Henrion et Dassy, 9
Henrion, Dassy & Heuschen, 32, 64
Herter's, 92
Higgins, J.C., 67, 86
High Standard, 49, 72
Hijos de Calixto Arrizabalaga, 36
Hijos de Echeverria, A., 29
Hijos de Aldazabal, Jose, 92
Hispano Argentina, 13
Hood Firearms Co., 44
Hopkins & Allen, 1, 10, 19, 68, 72, 78, 83
Hourat et Vie., 10
Howa Machinery, Ltd., 30
Hungarian military mark, 89
Hungarian proof, 31, 69, 91, 92, 93
Hunter, Hy, 4
Husqvarna, 51, 54
India proof, 54, 64, 76, 77
Industria Orbera, 36
Iranian military mark, 60
Iraola, Salaverria, 12
Israeli proof, 20, 24, 35, 43
Italian naval mark, 44
Italian proof, 51, 55, 57, 61, 62, 76, 89
Ithaca Gun Co., 41, 64, 73
Iver Johnson, 4, 24, 39, 41, 74, 78
Jacquemart, J., 3
Jager & Co., 27
Japanese military mark, 86
Jurras, Lee E., 75
Kind, Albrecht, 49, 86
Kirikale Tufek Fb., 21, 35, 68
Kodiak, 80
Kohout & Spol., 41
Kokura Arsenal, 65
Kolb, Henry M., 20, 67
Kommer, Theodor, 4, 27, 32
Krauser, A., 15
Krieghoff, H., 44, 49
Kriegskorte & Co., 20
Kure Arsenal, 44
L. Ancion-Marx, 31
L.E.S., 77
La Caruna Arsenal, 92
LA Distributers, 41
Langehan, Fritz, 30

Larranaga y Elartza, 13, 84
Lasagabaster Hermanos, 39
Lebeau-Courally, Auguste, 53
Liege United Arms Co., 81
Lignose, 33
Lithuanian military mark, 68
Maisuru Arsenal mark, 44
Maltby-Curtis Co., 5
Maltby-Henley Co., 4, 66
Mann, Fritz, 27, 41
Manurhin, 68
Marlin Firearms Co., 27, 39, 67, 79
Marlin, J.M., 20, 61
Masquelier, C.H., 85
Mauser, 13, 34
Mayor, E., 82
Mendoza, 27
Menz, August, 5, 9, 25
Meriden Firearms Co., 5, 66
Merkel, 73
Merwin, Hulbert & Co., 66, 67
Metallurgica Bresciana, 7
Mexican military mark, 92
Miroku Firearms Mfg., 21, 39, 70
Mossberg, O.F., 41
Mre. d'Armes Automatiques Bayonne, 22, 35
Mre. d'Armes des Pyrenees, 24, 25, 30, 32, 34, 36, 75, 85
Mre. d'Armes Le Page, 33, 49, 84
Mre. d'Armes des Pyrenees Francaise 3
Mre. Francais d'Armes et Cycles, 5
Mre. Liegeoise d'Armes a Feu, 56, 73
Mre. Stephanoise d'Armes, 21
Mugica, Jose Cruz, 50
Mukden Arsenal, 65
Nagoya Arsenal, 65
Navy Arms, 44
Noble Mfg. Co., 42
Norrahammer, 93
Oesterreichische Waffenfabrik, 11, 35
Oesterreichische Werke, 34
Ojanguren y Marcaide, 6
Ojanguren y Vidosa, 7, 63, 84
Orbea Hermanos, 3, 35
Ormachea, Fernando, 5

Ortgies, Heinrich, 6
Orueta Hermanos, 23
P.A.F., 50
Paatz, Bernhard, 38
Paraguayan military mark, 93
Parker Bros., 78
Parker-Hale, 15
Perazzi, 85
Perla gripmark, 33
Persian military mark, 88, 89
Peruvian military mark, 93
Phoenix Arms Co., 42
Pickert, Frederick, 6, 83
Pieper, 11, 20, 84
Polish military mark, 70
Portuguese mark 17
Portuguese military mark, 17, 53, 56, 66, 88
Portuguese Naval mark, 44, 45
Posumavska Zbrojovka, 28
Precise Imports Corp., 21
Puccinelli Company, 32
Reck Sportwaffenfabrik, 22, 32
Reising Mfg. Co., 80
Relay Products Ltd., 15, 75
Remington Arms Co., 13, 22
Remington, E. & Sons, 22
Renken et Fils, 58
Retolaza Hermanos, 1, 6, 33, 59, 67 75, 79
RG Industries, 42
Rheinmetall, 11
Rigarmi, 22
Rivolier Pere et Fils, 39
Robar et Cie., 21, 36
Robar et Dekerkhove, 11, 41
Rocky Mountain Arms Corp., 81
Rohm, 17, 18, 19, 20, 22, 23, 24, 42
Romerwerk, 15
Rossi, Amadeo, 6, 23
Roumanian mark, 54
Ruby Arms Co., 28
Russian mark, 20, 42, 43
Russian Military mark, 49
Russian proof, 19, 24, 25, 30, 38, 39, 40, 45, 64, 66, 90
Russian quality control mark, 7, 12, 30

Russian Tula proof mark, 31
Ryan, T.E., 23
S-M Corp., 50
Sabatti & Tanfoglio, 33
San Martin y Cia., 60
Santos, Modesto, 11
Sarasqueta, Victor, 82
Sasebo Arsenal, 45
Sauer, J.P. & Sohn, 6, 7, 28, 83
Savage Arms Corp., 83, 85
Schilling, V. Charles, 29, 85
Schmidt & Haberman, 18
Schwarzlose, A.W., 50
Schweitzer Industrie Gesellschaft 28,
Sears, Roebuck & Co., 6
Security Industries of America, 16
Sedgley, R.F., 23
Sharps Arms Co., 31, 81
Sheridan Products, 33
Siamese military mark, 69
Simson & Co., 33, 67
Smith & Wesson, 6, 23
Smith, L.C., 78
Smith, Otis A., 37
Soc. Espanola de Armas y Mun., 47 47
Soc. Espanola de Armas y Municiones 28, 47
Soc. Fr. Metallurgie/Mecanique, 42
Societe d'Armes, 11
Societe Francaise d'Armes, 11
South African proof, 28
Spandau Arsenal, 58
Spanish acceptance mark, 6
Spanish M1921 pistol mark, 27
Spanish police mark, 64
Spanish proof, 38, 41, 47, 50, 51, 53, 55, 56, 57, 58, 61, 64, 65, 67, 89, 90, 91, 92
Spesco, 18, 73
Springfield Arsenal, 73
Stenda Werk, 28, 33
Sterling Arms Co., 16
Stevens, J. Arms Co., 39
Steyr Daimler-Puch, 66
Stock, Franz, 35, 42
Stoeger Arms, 65, 74
Sturm, Ruger, 73

Suinaga y Aramperri, 6
Sweden mark, 31
Sweden proof, 14, 54, 65
Swiss military mark, 43, 48
Swiss police mark, 89
Swiss proof, 15, 68
Tallares Armas Livianas Arg., 68, 86
Tauler, 85
Taurus, 23
Thailand proof, 61
Thalmann, Ernst, 84
Thayer, Robertson & Cary, 64
Thompson/Center Arms, 7
Tiroler Waffenfabrik, 82
Tokyo Gas & Electric, 7
Tomas de Urizar y Cia., 36, 37
Tomiska, Alois, 68
Toriimatsu (Nagoya), 65
Toyokawa Arsenal, 45
Tradewinds, Inc., 21
Trejo, 86, 87
Triple-S Development Co., 34, 80
Trocaola y Aranzabal 26
Trocaola, Aranabal y Cia. 7
Trocaola, Aranzabal y Cia., 1, 7, 26
Tula Arsenal, 61, 65
Tula Weapons Factory, 40
Turner & Ross, 37
Tyrol, 72
U.S. mark, 3, 5, 7, 47, 88
U.S. Arms Corp., 72

Union Switch & Signal, 16
Universal Firearms Corp., 85
Valtion Kivaari Tehdas, 40
Venturini, 23
Venus Waffenwerk, 42
Verney-Carron, 29
Vilimec, A., 35
Vincitor, S.A., 1
Walther, Carl, 8, 12, 25, 36, 66
Walther, Lothar, 13
Warner Arms Corp., 16
Webley & Scott, 29, 49, 50, 63, 85
Weihrauch, Herman Sportwaffen, 17, 24
West German proof, 22, 33, 38, 45, 70, 71, 75, 81, 86, 90
Western Arms Corporation, 35
Wiener Waffenfabrik, 8, 39
Winchester Arms Co., 12, 16
Winslow Arms Co., 90
Woerther, E., 27
Yokasuka Arsenal, 45
Yugoslavian military mark, 62, 88, 90
Zaragoza, 8
Zbrojovka Brno, 41
Zbrojovka Praga, 28, 42
Zehner, E., 10
Zoli, A., 34
Zoli, Antonio, 46
Zulaica y Cia., 60, 79

Cumberland Trail Library System
Flora, Illinois 62839